CONSTANTINE ISSIGHOS

FOR GOD, COUNTRY
AND
DRUG PROHIBITION

NORTHWATER

Books by Constantine Issighos

My Six-Sided Log Home

The Magic World of In-Laid Pictorial Tapestry

Constantine Issighos: a Fibre Artist

For God, Country and Drug Prohibition

Prisoners of Our Ideals

Northwater is an imprint of Awaqkuna Books Inc.

www.awaqkunabooks.com

FOR GOD, COUNTRY

AND DRUG PROHIBITION

Library and Archives Canada

ISBN 978-0-9782018-7-6

Library and Archives Canada Cataloguing in Publication

This book was designed by the author.

"The Human Race is made of two kinds of humans – the dialectical intelligent human without religion, and the religious human without dialectical intelligence."

"Adults should be free to make lifestyle decisions without the intervention of the state."

2009 Landmark ruling of the Argentine Supreme Court
on possession of drugs.

CONTENTS

IN THE BEGINNING   1

1   A BRIEF HISTORY: CHRONOLOGY OF TOBACCO,
    ALCOHOL, DRUG SUBSTANCE & PROHIBITION   7
    Earliest Recorded Drug & Alcohol Use   8
    Earliest Drug Prohibition   11
    Earliest Alcohol Use & Prohibition   13
    Coffee & Tobacco Prohibition   16
    Prohibition Laws & Temperance Societies   18
    Brief List of Temperance Societies   22

2   NATURAL STIMULANTS   23
    Coca Leaf   25
    De-Cocainized Coca Leaf   28
    Marijuana   29
    Hashish   30
    Hashish-Oil   31
    Coffee - Caffeine   31
    Other Natural and Processed Stimulants   33

3   WHO IS USING RECREATIONAL DRUGS?   35
    Why Teenagers Use Drugs   38
    Persons Suffering FROM Post-traumatic Stress Disorder   39
    Marginalized People   39
    Recreational Drug Users   40
    Mental Patients   41

4 AMERICAN THEOCRACY AND PROHIBITION
   ALCOHOL & DRUGS   43

5 NATURE OF PROHIBITIONS   65

   Social Taboos   66
   Religious Morality anD Prohibition   66
   Temperance Movement   67
   Prohibition Under Blue Laws   69
   The Effects of Prohibitions: Quality of drugs   69
   Distribution of Illicit Drugs   71
   Legal Drug Regulations & Quality Control   72
   Prohibition of Heroin/Morphine   73

6 PROHIBITION: A PERSONAL AFFAIR   75

7 PHOTO TOUR OF FACTS & PROPAGANDA
          1820 - 1937   85

   Before Prohibition   87
   PRODUCTS Containing COCAINE   88
   Religious Propagated Temperance Movement
          1820-1920   93
   Drug Prohibition Propaganda   95
   Media Propaganda   96
   Coca Leaf Products   99

8 IN THE SHADOW OF DRUG PROHIBITION   101

   Victims and Casualties   116

9 WAR ON DRUGS: AN ANATOMY OF FAILURE   133

10 WAR ON DRUGS: THE HUMAN TRAGEDY   153

Militarization of Prohibition 157

The War Within: 1914 to Present 163

Calling the "Dogs of War" 172

11 STRONG ARM ECONOMICS
   ...FAIR TRADE OF COCA LEAF PRODUCTS 177

12 ECONOMICS AGAINST DRUG TRAFFICKING 193

Prevention 209

Crime reduction 210

13 IN PLAIN LANGUAGE:
   DRUG DECRIMINALIZATION 215

American Civil Liberties Union 216

Currently Illegal Drugs Have Not Always Been Illegal 216

Decades of Drug Prohibition: A History of Failure 217

Drug Prohibition is a Public Health Message 218

Drug Prohibition Creates More Problems than it Solves 219

Prohibition is a destructive Force in the Inner-City
Communities 220

Drugs Are Here To Stay - Let's Reduce Their Harm 220

Ending Prohibition Would Not Necessarily Increase Drug
Abuse 221

Transnational Institute: 222

Law Enforcement Against Prohibition 226

Harm Reduction Steps: Vancouver's InSite Program 227

Latin America Enacts Drug Decrinalization 229

Europe's Lenient Lands 231

INDEX 233

IN THE BEGINNING

This book is not an autobiography of my experience as a contrabandist, smuggler, bootlegger, forger and corruptor of officials. Although some details of my personal activities under prohibition are brought forward, those are to support certain points and thus are not the core essence of this book.

I try to show that drug use, distribution, production and policies cannot be examined in isolation from the politics and practices of Prohibition and the War on Drugs. History shows that prohibitive alcohol and drug policies more often than not were motivated by religious morality and politics rather than by public health concerns. In the last forty years the relationship between drugs and politics has been central to the controversy regarding the Drug Enforcement Agency (DEA) and US foreign policy involvement in the drug producing countries. This controversy between drug trafficking and the DEA is based on blurred and murky activities because that is the world of drug prohibition, trafficking, corruption and political crime.

For the last 200 years, religiosity and moral panic about alcohol and drugs have been linked with delusionally perceived threads of particular ethnic and visual minorities. Religious puritanical moralists have a perpetual conflict in dealing with sexual relations because sex, in the human world, is not an "immaculate" act in any form. The use of opium and cocaine were regarded as being evil largely because of the concern over sexual relations between white American women and Chinese or black men. Puritanical moralists were addressing primarily a white, native-born, middle-class audience. Religious organizers and moralists played down their denominational differences in order to concentrate on their main goal: recruiting female members for the revival of religious morality. Any sort of human vice or habit, such as gambling, pre-marital sex or smoking, would have served their purpose, but, they chose alchohol due to its popularity. Women's ever ready desire to have some control over men's perceived lack of responsible drinking was exploited by religious moralists who promoted their hidden agenda: political influence and power over setting public policies. In short, religious fundamentalists simply "highjack" the women's temperance movement and thus undermined the initial face of women's rights and feminism.

Early in the 20th century, prohibition was introduced over drugs and alcohol, creating a negative social condition that resulted in a human tragedy. Militarization of public policy, such as the infamous alcohol prohibitions of the 1920's was fought by guns and between smugglers and bootleggers against Treasury Law Enforcement agents. Gangsterism and corruption, extortion and murder were the tragic consequences felt by society. The more than 100 years of delusional advocacy of establishing a religious "moral" society, caused only 13 years of bloody internal conflict. But the war on drugs has caused worldwide human suffering, attempts of cultural genocide, and the imprisonment of millions of recreational drug users, addicts and drug producers. While legal and human rights abuse is caused by the DEA in the US, its militarized force in Latin America is a deadly assault against indigenous people. It is a hidden cultural genocide conducted by hired mercenaries, narco-terrorists, and right-wing paramilitary "death-squads" so that North Americans and Europeans can enjoyed their recreational and habitual cravings. Million of indigenous people have been uprooted from their traditional lands, either by the DEA's fumigation of coca leaves or by the drug traffickers who took over their traditional fruit and vegetable agricultural lands. Poverty, misery, sickness and hunger are the consequences of attempting to enforce America's second "noble experiment", the first being the Alcohol Prohibition of the 1920's.

No word description however vivid and no photograph however true, can give a clear concept of the overwhelming obstacles that had to be overcome to make the Andean Sierras of South America accessible and habitable. The rugged terrain of the mountain system of the Sierras, the harsh high-altitude climate and dense jungle vegetation, would appear to be fit only for producing and sustaining a backward, poverty stricken people. In such a geographical area of Peru, I first encountered simple down-to-earth *campesinos* with a long cultural history in the arts, architecture and medicinal cures. Coca leaves, Una de Gato and many other traditional medicines are an integral part of the Peruvian and Bolivian living legends. Coca leaves have been part of the indigenous diet for thousands of years. It is used for brewing tea and as a natural energy stimulant in beverage drinks, including Coca-Cola, Pepsi Cola, Red Bull Cola etc. They are the same coca leaves that the DEA is trying to eradicate and thus destroy a commercial and an ancient cultural product. So far, no rational arguments presented by Latin governments before the UN have been successful in showing that coca leaf is not cocaine.

The eradication of coca leaves is one facet of the war on drugs. Under the definition of "war"–which implies a sudden emergency, an imminent threat, the interruption of normal life and law-there can be no limit to the moral erosion of humanity. Under moral erosion, the irrational becomes a routine practice. For a self-proclaimed shining example of human rights and democracy, the US is funding mercenary armies to eradicate coca production in Peru, Bolivia, Colombia and parts of the Amazonian region of Brazil. Local and foreign mercenaries are normally attached to militarized police and regular army units, so they are not officially classified as mercenaries, death-squads or paramilitaries. Yet that is what they are, a proxy army of cut-throats prowling the Latin America jungles day and night, murdering, beating, raping, torturing and illegally detaining those who are suspected of coca cultivation or production of coca products. Tens of thousands of innocent campesinos have been killed, their families destroyed, their livelihood disrupted and their livestock poisoned in order to eradicate the coca plant. Little matter that the coca plant has been cultivated in those countries since time immemorial, and used as a healing medicine and pain reliever. The insane attempt to eradicate–rather than regulate–has proven every bit as profitable, as the militarized involvement of DEA and corrupt mercenaries now can play both sides. Drawing huge amounts of dollars for the "war on drugs", while also raking in bribes from the drug cartels to keep the trade thriving has led to the vast, pervasive corruption of government officials, and a level of criminality unprecedented in history.

Peru in the early 1990's was a country at war. Rebel forces of the Maoist Sendero Luminoso (Shining Path) and Tupac Amaru (MRTA) were conducting a bloody civil war against the government of Alan Garcia. Narco-terrorists operated in the jungle on behalf of the drug cartels. Against them were the militarized Peruvian police, regular army special forces units and their paid mercenaries. Assassinations and bombings were a common sight in villages, town and large cities like the capital of Lima. To make matters worse, the national government had difficulties in meeting its financial obligations with the International Monetary Fund (IMF). Economic policy was geared towards preserving foreign-exchange capital by nationalizing all private and business foreign currencies in Peruvian banks. In order to preserve its foreign capital, the Peruvian government imposed a blanket prohibition on the importation of all non-essential products. Industrial and chemical products, European and American liquor, cars and luxury goods were also placed under import prohibition. Importation of essential goods, such as dry-goods and grains were permitted, so long as the importer had his own foreign exchange to pay for them. Within a year, most foods in grocery stores began to deplete. People's panic caused hoarding of food and other essential items. The black market began to thrive, and by the second year of blanket prohibition, most consumer goods were provided illegally. Special custom units were patrolling the highways, sea ports and airports for contraband.

However, their aim was to steal part of the illegal goods, extort bribes or finance the next shipment of contrabands. Municipal units were patrolling local open markets (street vendors) for possible contraband. Often, those street vendors were permitted to do their daily business in exchange for a small bribe. Large scale smuggling, however, was done in foreign industrial and chemical products, American cigarettes, liquor from around the world and electronics. The relative few who were engaged in this level of smuggling and bootlegging were able to continue their illegal activities with the support of corrupt custom officials, army patrol officers and their police, and anti-drug units. The Peruvian "blanket-prohibition" became a profitable business for those who were capable of outsmarting their competition, bribing key officials or protecting their goods from bandits.

For little more than five years, I was involved in smuggling industrial goods and chemicals as well as European and North American liquor. Like others, I also began as a small-time smuggler. Luck and opportunity was on my side until I had accumulated enough foreign currency to pay bribes and to increase my illegal activities. Unlike others, I was not a Peruvian national nor was I familiar with the customs and manners of locals. But I learned fast! I undertook smuggling out of necessity, for I was robbed of my money and needed to survive. I travelled most of the interior and coastline of Peru and parts of the jungle of Bolivia in order to conduct my activities. It was during my travels that I encountered various anti-drug forces who were operating in the jungles against coca growers and coca-base producers. Circumstances brought me to local communities both before and after coca eradication. I witnessed the destructive effects that drug prohibition and blanket-prohibition imposed on Peruvian society. After five years as a contrabandist, bootlegger, corruptor and forger of documents, the destructive effects of prohibition is no longer an academic subject. The lessons to be learned are simple, for the end of prohibition means the end of criminality.

1

A BRIEF HISTORY: CHRONOLOGY OF TOBACCO, ALCOHOL, DRUG SUBSTANCE AND PROHIBITION

"That which is called sin in others
is experiment for us."

Ralph Waldo Emerson

The history of natural stimulants and processed drugs, such as alcohol, tobacco, coffee, opium and cannabis, and the use of alkaloid acids is completely entwined with human history. The uses and abuses of them goes back as far as recorded history. Plants containing opiates have been chewed (coca leaves, tobacco) and smoked almost as long as alcohol (beer, wine, spirits) has been imbibed. There are no actual records to give us a clear insight into the holistic/magical arts of drug used by the ancients who may have discovered them. The probable accidental discovery of their healing powers or their use as recreational drugs, the narcotic power of roots, barks, leaves and berries, may have occurred during earliest times. Fortunately, some early Temple medicine men and women were careful observers, and had a scientific bent or deep human compassion which they relied upon to search for a valid use of natural drugs. Prohibitions against recreational stimulants were also imposed upon the use of them at various stages in history. Prohibitions were imposed when ambitious leaders wanted to increase their power by controlling people's habits, desires and customs.

EARLIEST RECORDED DRUG & ALCOHOL USE

5000 B.C.
The Sumerians used poppy-opium, described it as 'joy".
3500 B.C.
Egyptian historical papyrus records of the production of alcohol and detailed descriptions of a brewery for beer and wine.
2500 B.C.
Historical evidence shows peasants of Switzerland eating poppy seeds.
c. 450 Babylonian Talmud
"Wine is at the head of all medicines; where wine is lacking, drugs are necessary".

300 B.C.
Theophrastus (371-287 B.C.)
Greek Naturalist and Philosopher
Provided undisputed reference/records to the use of poppy-drink.

250 B.C. Psalms, 104: 14-15
"Thou dost cause grass to grow for the cattle and plants for man to cultivate, that he may bring forth food from the earth, and wine to gladden the heart of man".

c. 1000
Opium is widespread and used in China and the Far East.

c. 1525
Paracelsus (1490-1541)
Introduces laudanum or tincture of opium into medical practice.

1619
America's first marijuana law was enacted at Jamestown Colony of Virginia. It was the law obligating all farmers to grow Indian hemp. Over the next 200 years hemp was legal tender and a critical crop for a number of purposes - ropes, incense, cloth and canvas, cordage for baling cotton, and until the early 1800's as a recreational drug. The United States census of 1850 recorded 8,327 hemp farms of 2,000-acres per farm.

1680
Thomas Syndenham (1625-1680)
"Among the remedies which it has pleased the Almighty God to give to man to relieve his sufferings, none is so universal and efficacious as opium".

1690
English Law is enacted: "Act for the Encouraging of the Distillation of Brandy and Spirits from Corn".

1792
Samuel Taylor Coleridge writes "Kubla Khan" while under the influence of opium.

1805
Friedrich W. A. Serturner, German chemist, isolates and creates morphine.
1841
Dr. Jacques J. Morean uses the drug hashish in treatment of mental patients at the Bicetre.
1844
Avant-garde Parisian artist and writers develop their own cannabis ritual, leading to the establishment of "Le Club de Haschischins" (The Club of Hashish users).
1844
Cocaine is isolated in its pure form from coca leaves.
1868
Dr. George Wood, professor of medicine at the University of Pennsylvania and author of "The Treatise on Therapeutics" on the effects of opium: "A sensation of fullness is felt in the head, soon to be followed by a universal feeling of delicious ease and comfort, with an elevation and expansion of the whole moral and intellectual nature, which is, I think, the most characteristic of its effects…and the capacity to act, and to bear fatigue, is greatly augmented."
1883
Dr. Theodor Aschenbrandt, a German army physician, secures a supply of pure cocaine from the pharmaceutical firm of Marck, issues it to Bavarian soldiers during their manoeuvres, and reports on the beneficial effects of the drug in increasing the soldiers' ability to endure fatigue.
1885
The Report of the Royal Commission on Opium concludes that "opium is more like the westerner's liquor than a substance to be feared and abhorred."
1889
John Hopkins Hospital in Baltimore, Maryland, is established. One of its founders, Dr. William S. Halstead, is a morphine user throughout his successful surgical career lasting until his death in 1922.

1894

The British Government's Report of the Indian Drug Commission, Seven Vol. is published. It concludes that: "There is no evidence of any weight regarding the mental and moral injuries from the moderate use of these drugs…Moderation does not lead to excess in hemp [marijuana] any more than it does in alcohol. Regular, moderate use of ganja [slang for marijuana] or bhang produces the same effects as moderate and regular doses of whiskey."

1898

Synthesized heroin [Diacetylmorphine] is produced in Germany. It is proclaimed to be a "safe preparation free from addiction-forming properties"

EARLIEST DRUG PROHIBITION

Too often during the early years of prohibition, the use and harmful effect of illicit drugs were exaggerated. Drug abuse, however, shows its inevitable harm in the immune system. Drug prohibition, on the other hand, is not a medical solution. It must be said that the enforcement of the National Prohibition Act was a bad start that has affected millions of drug addicts and recreational users. The first Pure Food and Drug Act became a Prohibition Law; until its enforcement, it was possible to buy, in stores or by mail order, medicines containing morphine, cocaine or heroin without their being labelled by such terms.

1909

The US Congress passes a law that prohibits the importation of smoking opium.

1910

Dr. Hamilton Wright, considered by some the father of US drug abolitionist laws, reports that American estate contractors give cocaine to their black workers to get more work out of them.

1914
Dr. Edward H. Williams cites Dr. Christopher Kochs [in the New York Times, Feb. 9] "Most of the attack upon white women of the South are the direct result of the cocaine crazed Negro brain."

1918
The Harrison Narcotic Act is enacted, controlling the sale of opium, opium derivatives and cocaine.

1920
The US Department of Agriculture publishes a brief document urging Americans to cultivate marijuana as a profitable enterprise.

1930
The Federal Bureau of Narcotics is formed. Many of its agents, including its first commissioner Henry J. Anslinger are former prohibition temperance members.

1930-1937
A number of films are financed by religious groups and produced as morality tales attempting to influence youth about the moral dangers of cannabis use. They are, *"Reefer Madness"* [1936], *"Marijuana"* [1936], *"Assassin of Youth"* [1937], *"Party Girl"* [1930], *"Damaged Lives"* [1930], *'The Road to Ruin"* [1934], *"Gambling with Souls"* [1936], and *"The Cocaine Friends"* [1936].

EARLIEST ALCOHOL USE & PROHIBITION

Since ancient times, the prohibition of alcohol, drugs, certain foods, or *"blanket prohibition"* was imposed on people by political legislation or religious laws. In all cases, prohibition was, and still is, a social phenomenon used as a common means of attempting to control or enforce any social taboo. Prohibitions existed and still exist at various levels of government or other authorities, from ancient to the present times. Any legal legislation that forbids something is a prohibition by its very nature. Such legal legislation can prohibit a specific act or product or can be a "blanket prohibition" against, for example, the importation of non-essential goods into a country. While I was residing in Peru in the 1990s, the government had imposed a "blanket-prohibition" on all foreign products in its attempt to support national industries and to avoid meeting its foreign financial obligations. The prohibited products, such as alcohol, cigarettes and coffee, generally continued to be available through the blackmarket, by prescription, or through smuggling or bootlegging. At present times, most Islamic countries prohibit the consumption of alcohol. Other countries, including the Soviet Union (1914-1925), Norway (1916-1927), Canada, Iceland (1915-1922), Finland (1919-1932) and the United States (1920-1933), have had alcohol prohibition.

2000 B.C.
An Egyptian temple priest prohibitionist commands his followers "I, thy superior, forbid thee to go to the taverns. Thou art degraded like a beast".

350 B.C. Proverbs 31 : 6-7
"Give strong drink to him who is perishing, and wine to those in bitter distress; let them drink and forget their poverty, and remember their misery no more."

4th Century
St. John Chrysostom [345-407 A.D.]
"I hear man cry. Would there be wine! O folly! O madness! Is it wine that causes this abuse? No, for if vou say. Would there were no light!"

1639-1723
Increase Mather: "Drink is in itself a creature of God, and to be received with thankfulness...The wine is from God, but the drunkard is from the Devil." Early signs of the propagation of religious Temperance Movement.

1736
The Gin Act in England is enacted. Its avowed object was for this popular spirit to 'become so dear to the consumer that the poor will not be able to launch into excessive use of them' This effort results in widespread organized bootlegging and a steady rise in the consumption of adulterated alcohol.

1745-1813
Benjamin Rush, a medical physician in Philadelphia, publishes a book in 1784 entitled *An Inquiry into the Effects of Ardent Spirits upon the Human Mind and Body.* He is regarded as the father of temperance ideology.

1790
Dr. Benjamin Rush, of the Philadelphia College of Physicians, persuades his associates to convey an appeal to the US Congress to " impose such heavy duties upon all distilled spirits as shall be effective to restrain their intemperate use in the country."

1845
A law prohibiting the public sale of liquor is enforced in New York State. It was repealed in 1847.

1901
The US Senate adopts a resolution to prohibit the sale of opium and alcohol by American traders " to aboriginal tribes and uncivilized races." It also extended to include uncivilized elements in America itself and its territories, such as Indians, Alaskans, Hawaiians, railroad workers, and immigrants at ports of entry.

1914

US Congressman Richard P. Hobson of Alabama urged an alcohol prohibition amendment to the Constitution proclaiming "Liquor will actually make a brute out of a Negro, causing him to commit unnatural crimes. The effects are the same on the white man, though the white man being further evolved, it takes a longer time to reduce him to the same level."

1929

About one gallon of denatured industrial in ten is diverted into bootlegged liquor by adulterating it with methyl [wood] alcohol. About 40 Americans per million die each year from drinking poisonous illegal alcohol. Adulteration of alcohol, drugs or food under "blanket-prohibition" is a common phenomenon, due to the lack of any government regulated quality control.

1932

In this year alone, approximately 45,000 people received jail sentences for alcohol offences under prohibition laws. During the first eleven years of the prohibition Volstead Act, nearly 18,000 persons were employed by the Prohibition Bureau; of those 11,983 were terminated "without prejudice" and 1,606 were terminated for bribery, extortion, theft, falsification of criminal records, forgery or perjury.

Present Day

In Pakistan and Saudi Arabia, the production, transportation, sale and consumption of alcohol is strictly prohibited. As a result, alcohol smuggling and bootlegging is widespread.

COFFEE & TOBACCO PROHIBITION

In 1575, Mexican religious authorities in Spanish America exhibited the first recorded prohibition of tobacco use. Bearing in mind their faith and the time period in which they lived, missionaries were extremely bigoted towards the indigenous Indians. They believed that the signs of a true conversion were not only that the Indians adhered to the doctrines of the Catholic Church, but that they also completely give up their habitual smoking. Punishment against tobacco use was increased as Indians did not regard smoking as a sign of paganism. When the Indians came into the church, smoking for all the world as if they were at a pagan ceremony, they were met with the most severe ecclesiastical disapproval. In 1588 Peru, by decree of the Provincial Council in Lima, penalties against tobacco use included death.

The earliest coffee prohibition is said to have occurred in the Ottoman Empire during the rule of Sultan Murat IV from 1625 to 1640. It is said that the paranoid Murat IV often walked the city of Istanbul disguised in order to hear what the people were saying about him. Every time Murat IV stopped by a tavern, he heard men singing and watched them getting drunk. However, when he moved on to a coffee house and saw the customers drinking coffee and engaging in political conversations about the dreadful state of the empire, he was not happy at all. He suspected that it was the coffee they were drinking that caused them to think and talk about the sorry state of affairs. The coffee drinkers were blaming Murat himself for all of the Ottoman Empire's social ills. The Sultan, clearly upset, went back to his palace to think. He compared alcohol drinking to coffee drinking, and to people's subsequent behaviour. Murat concluded that it was the coffee that caused people to become intoxicated. Men who were in coffee houses were thinking and saying bad things about the Empire. Men who were in taverns drinking alcohol were getting drunk and were singing. Above all, Murat noticed that coffee drinkers were also smokers, which he associated with coffee houses. Murat was known to walk the streets of Istanbul with an executioner, ordering the beheading of anyone he saw drinking coffee and smoking. It is reported that during his rule, from 1625 to 1640, between 10,000 and 20,000 people were executed during his purge of coffee and smoking.

c. 1493
The use of tobacco is introduced into Spain by Cristobal Colon and his crew upon returning from the Americas.

c. 1613
John Rolf, the husband of the famous Indian Pocahontas, sends the first commercial shipment of Virginia tobacco from Jamestown to England.

16th Century
Coffee was introduced into Europe by an Austrian merchant who witnessed coffee drinking in the Ottoman Empire (Turkey). When the Ottomans were retreating from the Austro-Hungarian Empire in the 16th century, they left behind bags of coffee beans. Not knowing what those beans were, the Austrians were destroying them until the merchant asked and was granted permission to collect them. He roasted them, ground them, percolated them, and opened the first coffee house in Europe. Coffee's active alkaloid–caffeine–is a natural stimulant that affects cardiac hormones.

c. 17th Century
Friedrich, vassal of the Prince of Waldeck, paid 10 thalers to anyone who snitched on a coffee drinker.

c. 1650
Tobacco prohibition is enforced in the states of Bavaria, Saxony and in Zurich. However, tobacco prohibition is ineffective. The ruler, Sultan Mural IV of the Ottoman Empire imposes the death penalty on anyone smoking and drinking coffee. The punishment included beheading, hanging, quartering or crushing the smoker's hand and feet. It is reported that more than 100,000 people lost their lives. In spite

of all the horrors of public persecutions, the habit of smoking and coffee drinking still persisted.

1691
In Luneburg, Germany, the penalty for smoking tobacco was death.

1912
The editor of *Century* magazine proclaims "The relation of tobacco, especially in the form of cigarettes, and alcohol and opium is the logical regular series...There is no energy more destructive of soul, mind, and body, or more subversive of good morals than the cigarette. The fight against the cigarette is a fight for civilization."

1921
Cigarettes are illegal in 14 US states and 92 anti-cigarette bills are pending in 28 states. Young women are expelled from college for smoking cigarettes.

1936
The Pan-American Coffee Bureau is organized to promote coffee in the US.

2004
The Kingdom of Bhutan declares the sale of tobacco illegal. This is followed by the smuggling and **blackmarket** availability of tobacco products. By 2006, tobacco is the most commonly seized illicit drug in the Kingdom.

PROHIBITION LAWS & TEMPERANCE SOCIETIES

Beer, wine and whiskey were common on ships carrying colonists from Europe to the New World. Carrying on with European custom, most colonists drank alcohol regularly from an early age. Drinking, in fact, was the key to social gatherings. Following the American Revolution (1775-1783), distilled spirits such as whiskey became important commercial goods for the up and coming business class. By this time, the Old

World custom of drinking large quantities of alcohol was widespread throughout the American landscape. Thus, concern about alcohol consumption existed from the nation's birth. A large sector of the American business class wanted sober and healthy workers for their manufacturing industries. They were predominantly religious puritan evangelical Protestants who were in opposition to the sale and consumption of alcoholic drinks. They were even opposed to public dancing. By the end of 1810, a radical ideological temperance movement developed, which was well organized and financed by rich men and women. These temperance societies consisted of many religious denominations who shared a common Puritanical goal: they believed in establishing "God's Kingdome on Earth." More later.

1789
The first *American Temperance Society* is formed in Litchfield, Connecticut.

1826
The *American Society for the Promotion of Temperance* is founded in Boston. It is estimated that by 1833 there were 6,000 local temperance societies, with more than one million members. These members promoted their interest in spreading religion, their version of morality and social taboos.

1834
In New Zealand, the first recorded temperance meeting is held in the Bay of Islands, Northland.

1838
In Ireland, a Catholic priest, Theobald Mathew, persuades thousands of men to sign a pledge of drinking abstinence, thus establishing the *Teetoral Abstinence Society.*

1852
The *Woman's States Temperance Society* of New York is the first such society formed for and run by women. They are ardent prohibitionists.

1869

The *Prohibition Party* is formed, headed by Gerrit Smith, twice an abolitionist candidate for President of the US.

1872

In Australia, the *"Sons of Temperance"* is formed to promote abstinence from alcohol.

1874

The *Woman's Christian Temperance Union is* formed in Cleveland.

1876

In England, *The League of the Cross* is founded as a Catholic total abstinence organization. It is closely associated with the British Women's Temperance Association, which was formed to persuade men to stop drinking.

1880

The *Department of Scientific Temperance Instruction in Schools and Colleges* is founded. Its main objective is to coerce the moral suasion of students "we must first be convinced that alcohol and kindred narcotics are by nature outlaws, before they will outlaw them."

1882

The *Personal Liberty League of the United States* was founded to opposes the increasing public momentum for compulsory abstinence from alcohol.

1883

Frances Willard forms the *World's Woman's Christian Temperance Union.*

1885

In Sri Lanka, the temperance movement of *"Sure Virodhi Vyaparaya"* is seen by the British colonial rulers as a direct attack on their regime which rents out drinking taverns to get revenue for government treasures.

1886

US Congress enacts a law making "temperance education" mandatory in all public schools including schools in all territories and on military and naval bases.

1898

In Ireland, James Cullen founds *the Pioneer Total Abstinence Association.*

1918

The *Methodist Episcopal Church Board of Temperance, Prohibition and Public Moral* is founded. It is a major organization in the American temperance movement which leads to the introduction of prohibition in 1920.

1918

The 18th Amendment, establishing National Prohibition, is enacted.

1918

The Anti-Saloon League is founded under the influence of the Episcopal religious coalition.

1926

An ardent supporter of alcohol prohibition is the notorious KKK, led by racist Rev.Branford Clark. It runs posters proclaiming *"The Defence of the 18th Amendment".*

1920-1933

For 13 years, the legalized prohibition of alcohol/drugs is viewed by religious zealots and their right-wing followers as the magical solution to America's poverty, crime, violence and other social ills. American religiosity was similar to the German mentality of delusional beliefs that made the rise of Nazi power possible in the 1930's. Believing (not investigating) was the motto of extremism on both sides of the Atlantic Ocean. One can see the same delusional thinking in the social reactionaries who formed the 2009 *"Tea Party"* campaigns. Church celebrations in New York prior to Prohibition in 1920 said, "Let the church bells ring and let there be great rejoicing, for an enemy has been overthrown and victory grows the forces of righteousness".

1949

The social philosopher Ludwig von Mises best expressed his idea of personal liberty and freedom of choice as follows:

"Opium and morphine are certainly dangerous, habit-forming drugs. But once the principle is admitted that it is the duty of government to protect the individual against his/her own foolishness, no serious objection can be advanced against further encroachments. A good case could be made out in favor of the prohibition of alcohol and nicotine. And why limit the government's benevolent providence to the protection of the individual's body only? Is it not the harm a man can infect on his mind and soul even more disastrous than any bodily evils? Why not prevent him from reading bad books and seeing bad plays, from looking at all bad...[blaming they were] done by narcotic drugs."

BRIEF LIST OF TEMPERANCE SOCIETIES

❖ Anti-cigarette League of America

❖ Christianity and Alcohol

❖ International Organization of America

❖ The Hallelujah Trail

❖ Washington Movement

❖ World League Against Alcoholism

❖ Templars of Honor and Temperance

❖ The Catholic Total Abstinence Union of America

❖ Daughters of Temperance

2

NATURAL STIMULANTS

"Under the pressures of the cares and sorrows of our mortal condition, men have at all times, and in all countries, called in some physical aid to their moral consolation – wine, beer, opium, brandy, or tobacco."

Edmund Burke (1729-1797)

Natural stimulants contain chemical compounds that modify the way the body and brain work. Most processed drugs or natural stimulants create biological activities that can help or heal sick people. A relevant point is that there are no known natural or processed drugs that are not harmful or even poisonous when taken at high doses. It is for this reason that scientists work on drugs to discover the levels of toxic doses.

Understanding the concept of drugs is to understand that the term "drugs" has acquired a negative connotation since the "war on drugs" was declared in the 1960's. The public's negative view has been re-enforced by the widespread abuse of substances that are used for non-medical reasons and have become a serious sociological problem. In the natural balance of things, drugs have positive and negative effects on the body and mind. They can benefit as well as harm the nervous system, and have been part of medical advances in the way modern doctors treat diseases. It lived in South America for several years, and witnessed *curanderos*, *shaman* and holistic tribal doctors who treating 'evil spirits' of the mind and diseases of the body. Treatment in both cases are conducted in a similar way to what modern psychiatrists and physicians do today. Drugs are used in both instances and there is no health benefit without potential toxicity. There is no absolute "good" or "bad" about drugs. In western societies, we ritually follow the doctor's advice and suggestions, believing that he/she will cure our sickness. In the Latin World, the *campesinos* follow the ritualistic advice of the *curanderos* or holistic "medical" men. I have witnessed natural cures that were generally far too toxic for the sick person to survive. The point is that whether drugs are administrated in a natural or in a processed form, they still contain a level of toxicity within them.

COCA LEAF

Coca leaves are one of the world's most powerful natural stimulants. South American Indians of the highlands of the Andean Sierras mountains have been chewing coca leaves for at least 5000 years. Chewing coca leaves has been part of their medicinal, mystical and religious activities. Shamans *curanderos* from the traditional Sierras Indian tribes still smoke coca leaves for magical purposes. Inhaling the sacred vapors induces a trance-like state. It is believed that coca smoking enables a Shaman to cross "the bridge of smoke", and enter the world of spirits. It also activates his magical and curative powers against diseases. Because of the lack of oxygen at high altitutes, coca leaves have also been chewed as a breathing stimulant. Indian and foreign travelers describe that the Sierras mountain journey is less stressful when chewing coca leaves. Brewing coca leaves, Mate de Coca, is an energy stimulant used by most travellers who are not accustomed to high altitudes. Drinking coca tea tends to soothe the stomach; it is good for digestive problems. It is also less likely to induce jitteriness than caffeine. Other natural digestive stimulants are chamomile tea, green tea, ginger tea, Greek mountain tea and others. Chinese, Middle Eastern, Arabian, South American, East Indian and British cultures have a variety of natural stimulants made from tea leaves. These can be purchased in health stores, open markets, ethnic oriented shops and supermarkets in tea-bag style. Mate de Coca tea bags are a common product sold openly in supermarkets or in loose form in open markets of Peru, Bolivia, Ecuador etc. Restaurants and tea shops throughout South America serve Mate de Coca tea to adults and children. During my years living in Peru I often traveled to the Sierras region. I enjoyed brewing coca leaves for tea because I found it very helpful with my breathing. High altitude sickness (Soroche) can cause severe shortage of breath, headaches and dizziness. Coca leaves are a natural stimulant that alleviate those symptoms.

The popularity of using coca leaves was a widespread phenomenon during the 19th century in both the Americas and Europe. Coca leaves were the main ingredients in popular wines and drinks, including the widespread Coca Cola brand. In Europe, the famous Mariani Wine was a very popular coca-wine with the upper class, royalty and religious leaders. The Catholic Pope Leo XIII (1878-1903) enjoyed the invigorating properties of coca leaves. So much so, that the Pope awarded a Vatican gold metal to its distinguished originator, Angelo Mariani. In Britain the Peruvian Coca Wine was advertised for its qualities against fatigue of the mind and body, neuralgia, sleeplessness and despondency. In Atlanta, John Stith Pemberton (1831-1888) was the inventor of the Coca Cola beverage. He grew up in a European culture and attended public schools in Rome, Italy, where his parents lived for many years. He studied botanical principals, herbal remedies andways to purify the body of toxins. In 1870 Pemberton returned to the USA and became a permanent resident of Atlanta, Georgia. A few years before Coca Cola began its impressive rise to international acclaim, an alcoholic drink known as Pemberton's French Wine Coca was widelyspread throughout the state of Georgia. The demand for the tasty beverage was quite high. Pemberton's French Coca Wine was based on the European Vin Mariani formula mix of coca leaves and red wine, perfected in 1863 by Mariani & Co. of Paris, France. The Vin Mariani was successfully marketed in Europe and had been the world's only standard mixed formula of erythroxylon coca. Back in Atlanta, the future inventor of Coca-Cola and creator of the French Wine Coca describes his very popular wine:

"It is composed of an extract from the leaf of Peruvian Coca, the purest wine, and the Kola nut. It is the most excellent of all tonics, assisting digestion, imparting energy to the organs of respiration, and strengthening the muscular and nervous system"

Kola nut works as a stimulant as it is full of caffeine. Kola nut extract is used to reduce tiredness, hunger and aid digestion. It is very similar to the stimulant effects of a mug of strong coffee or tea. By 1886, the city fathers of Atlanta were influenced and pressured by the religious puritans of the Temperance Movement. These religious puritans wanted to create a society as they imagined or idealised it in accordance with their religious delusions. They simply wanted a "dry" public and they were willing to use their political power to enforce it. Their political power was so great that the city of Atlanta adopted the first legally imposed Alcohol Prohibition (1885) in the USA. Among other things, it prohibited the production, distribution and sale of wine. Forced out of the wine business, Pemberton decided to make use of another version of his popular drink. He simply dropped the wine and replaced it with sugar syrup, while keeping intact the coca formula. He invented the name "Coca-Cola" to identify his new beverage. With the aid of the coca leaves, the new non-alcoholic drink was praised for its beneficial effects on the mind and body. Members of the Temperance Movement were among those who praised the new drink.

In the meantime, in Albany NY, Lloyd Manufacturing Co. was marketing Cocaine Toothache Drops as an instantaneous cure. Another cocaine stimulant was the Coca-Bola chewing gum which both the Queen Victoria and Winston Churchill enjoyed. Sigmund Freud, father of contemporary psychology, enjoyed coca-based stimulants and also prescribed them to his patients. In fact, Freud treated his own depression with a cocaine-based stimulant. He reported feeling

"...exhilaration and lasting euphoria, which is in no way differs from the normal euphoria of the healthy person...You perceive an increase in self-control and possess more vitality and capacity for work...In other words, you are simply more normal, and it is soon hard to believe that you are under the influence of a drug." (Ernest Jones, The Life and Work of Sigmund Freud, Vol. 1, p.82)

Humans have always looked to use some type of stimulant to stress relieve, and tiredness or as an aid for relaxation. People who work especially long and hard hours may take a drink when arriving home as a stimulant or a relaxant from the day's stress. Stimulant drinks are used today to increase one's energy capacity in sports. Caffeine, which is a stimulant drug, is legally used in those energy drinks.

DE-COCAINIZED COCA LEAF

De-cocainized coca extract is widely used today in the beverage industry in both Europe and the USA. The de-cocainizing process means the cocaine alkaloid has be removed from the coca leaf to its lowest possible level, which is 0.4 to 0.13 micrograms. Red Bull Cola is a popular energy drink, which is full of caffeine and contains 0.4 micrograms of cocaine per litre. At this level, Red Bull Cola energy drinks do not pose a perceived threat of cocaine addiction. The company uses de-cocainized coca leaf extract in their product. This is not uncommon within the soft-drink industry. De-cocainized coca leaf extracts are used as a flavouring agent in foodstuffs around the world and are considered to be safe by the American DEA and the Council of Europe. Red Bull Cola, Pepsi Cola and Coca-Cola products all contain traces of micrograms of cocaine which remain in the extract after the de-cocainizing process. The use of coca leaves is something that the food industry is a bit coy about, given its links to cocaine–even if de-cocainized coca extracts are legal in most countries. So much so, that the Coca Cola company refuses to confirm or deny whether it uses either natural or de-cocainized coca extracts in its products. Although coca leaves are specifically classified as illegal, a special accommodation exists for "de-cocainized" coca, which is found in commercial products such as coca candy, coca chocolate, coca toothpaste, energy drinks etc. Interestingly enough, its uses outside the soft-drink industry was also behind the 1980's "inka-tea" mini scandal in the US. Shops were found to be carrying natural coca leaf tea bags–rather than de-cocainized–which contained alkaloid coca after testing; they were promptly removed from the shelves. In the catch-22 situation, coca leaf tea bags which are legal under a blurry notion of "de-cocainized" do not specify any maximum alkaloid content per tea bag weight. Coca leaves packed in teabag form that are for one serving–roughly one gram of leaves–would be under this limit. This is a very delicate legal classification, and recent commercial developments of the coca trade still need to be pushed ahead with legally regulating alkaloid content per weight.

MARIJUANA

Marijuana is a popular plant smoked for recreational reasons around the world. In the US alone, it is estimated that over 100 million American have tried marijuana, with more than 25 million using it in 2010. Marijuana, cannabis or hemp plant is one of the oldest non-processed psychoactive drugs known to humanity. A native of central Asia, cannabis may have been cultivated as long as ten thousand years ago. In China, it was cultivated in 4000 B.C. and in Turkestan by 3000 B.C. Cannabis has been used as a medicine in China, South America, Southeast Asia, South Africa and India. It has been used as a medical cure for malaria, constipation, and rheumatic pains; to lower fevers; to induce sleep; cure dysentery and for many other reasons. For religious and mystical purposes, hemp was also used during childbirth and depression. Hemp oil was used for treating of coughs, venereal disease and urinary incontinence. Today medical research continues in order to convince law makers of the medical benefits of marijuana.

Natural stimulants are chemical compounds that modify the way our body and mental state functions. Natural and processed stimulants can be harmful or even poisonous at high doses, and much of today's scientific investigation of drugs is geared to discover the gap between effective and toxic doses. It is known, however, that as there are no stimulant benefits without potential toxicity, there is no absolute goodness about drug stimulants. In a natural balance of opposites, their enormous health benefits outweigh the drawbacks in individual cases. Caffeine, for example, is good for bodily energy. Over - indulging in caffeine, however, may increase health risks for persons having a rapid heartbeat. The acceptance and rejection of marijuana use, its legalization or prohibition, its relation to drug trafficking or free market trade, are themes propounded by users around the world. The decision by the US Congress to pass the 1937 Marijuana Tax Act was based on testimonies derived from articles in newspapers owned by William Randolph Hearst, who had a significant financial interest in the forest industry, which manufactured his newsprint. This put him in direct competition with the hemp market which was gaining popularity with wood pulp producers. Deliberately, Hearst associated marijuana with hemp in his newspapers and film industry. He published many falsehoods fabricated to influence law makers. In addition, Hearst played a major part in outlawing marijuana, leading to its prohibition in the Marijuana Tax Act of 1937, legislation which also effectively outlawed hemp. It is now known that Hearst's business empire owned thousands of acres of timber forest and a large number of pulp mills to manufacture paper for his newsprint. The timber pulp industry was seen as being threatened by hemp, which yields 4.1 times more pulp than timber wood-pulp per acre. Hemp has an additional advantage over timber, since it can be re-grown yearly. The ban on the cultivation of hemp affected Hearst's strong financial involvement with timber logging and the newsprint industry.

HASHISH

Hashish is a natural stimulant commonly known as hash. It is the most potent part of the cannabis plant. It is produced by collecting and selecting the most potent material (THC) that the female marijuana plant generates. This most potent part of cannabis is Trichones, fine outgrowth or appendages on plants that generates a sticky resin. Other plants have this as well. For example, the sticky gum of the maple tree is maple resin. In hashish, it is obtained by collecting the trichomes from the flower tops of the female cannabis plant. After being collected, the trichomes are then pressed into a collective mass known as hashish. The collective trichomes are forced together under pressure. What makes hashish more potent than marijuana is that hashish concentrates the THC and eliminates most other plant material found in the cannabis plant. Most of the hashish now produced and made available to the public is often mixed with inert filler material that increases the weight and thus lowers its purity.

HASHISH-OIL

Hashish oil, commonly known as hash-oil, is a cannabis extract from hashish or marijuana. It is a thick liquid which is processed in solvents, such as petroleum ether, acetone, butane or alcohol. The end-product is separated from the hashish or marijuana plant, and the extract that remains is a concentrated form of cannabis. Depending on the refining process, the colour of hash-oil can range from white to dark. The lighter the colour, the higher the potency. The colour range is white, honey, light-brown, dark-brown, green or red.

COFFEE - CAFFEINE

It is not difficult to find varieties of coffee beans and coffee shops anywhere in the world. For example, coffee beans are rosted, and made for instant or de-caffeinated coffee. In some countries, such as Japan, there are shops selling cans of premade coffee drinks. There are literally millions of vending machines in Japanese cities that sell coffee in disposable cans. Caffeine is the coffee's main active ingredient. Caffeine removal from coffee beans is a de-caffeinating process, similar to de-cocainizing process of coca leaves. The de-caffeinating process removes the main active ingredients from the natural coffee bean in order to be used in many other products. The soft-drink and pharmaceutical industries are the main users. Within the healthcare industry, caffeine is classified and widely recognized as belonging in the same category of drugs as cocaine and amphetamines. They are all stimulant drugs. The only difference between caffeine drug and cocaine/amphetamine is that the drug caffeine is legal, while cocaine and amphetamine are not. Cocaine was made illegal in 1914, and amphetamines were outlawed in the 1950's. Tea made from coca leaves has the same effect as caffeine based soft drinks. According to the National Related Products (USA), soft drinks contain the following amount of caffeine in micrograms per 12 oz cans compared to the amount found in cups of coffee and tea, or a piece of chocolate.

Sugar-Free Mr. Pibb	58.8 mgs	Drip Coffee	115-175
Mountain Dew	55.0 mgs	Espresso 1.5 oz	100
Diet Mountain Dew	55.0 mgs	Brewed	80-135
Mello Yello	52.8 mgs	Instant	65-100
Coca Cola	45.6 mgs	Decaf, brewed	3-4
Diet Cola	45.6 mgs	Decaf, instant	2-3
Pepsi Cola	37.2 mgs	Tea, instant	30
Diet Pepsi	35.4 mgs	Ice-tea (120oz)	70
Shasta Cola	44.4 mgs	Tea, brewed	40
Shasta Cherry Cola	44.4 mgs	Chocolate 1oz	8-25
Shasta Diet Cola	44.4 mgs		
Dr. Pepper	39.6 mgs		
RC Cola	36.0 mgs		
Canada Dry	30.0 mgs		
Canada Dry (Diet)	1.2 mgs		
7Up	0 mgs		

OTHER NATURAL AND PROCESSED STIMULANTS

Absinthe
Alcohol
Amphetamine
Barbituates
Benzodiazepines
Cialis
Chloral-Hydrate
Cocaine
Dimethy Hryptamine (DMT)
Ectacy (MDMA)
GHB (gamma Hydroxybutyrate)
Heroin
Katamine (Ketalar)
Levitra (Vardenafil)
LSD (Hysergic acid diethylamide)
Mescaline
Morphine
Mushrooms-(psychoactive)
PCP (Phencyclidine)
Quaulude (Methaqualose)
STP (DOM)
Steroids
Viagra

The history of drug-stimulants is shrouded in the beginning of the human race. From time immemorial, alcohol–wine or beer– has been used by humans to get intoxicated. Tobacco, hemp/cannabis, hashish, opium poppy and coca leaves were consumed to get relief from life's stress and for medical reasons. Some stimulants were smoked, chewed or brewed throughout human history. Today, stimulants are consumed as a defence mechanism against the impersonal lifestyle most people live; religion and false spiritualism has led to monolithic beliefs, and "morality" has been peddled as a magical cure for all social ills. In the last 150 years, Temperance advocates have also entered us into the acrimonious debate about stimulants–including alcohol–that we are still facing today. The uses and effects of drugs, therefore, have been given a bad-rap that has distorted their benefits. One must remember that during our origins we never were given a blueprint to guide us on morality, good, evil, love, hate or on the use and abuse of drugs. We had to discover things by trial and error. In our social path, superstition, taboos, irrational fears, religions, cults and cultural habits have motivated us to come to many irrational conclusions. We humans have discovered drug-stimulants as we roamed the landscape in search of food and shelter. Our greatest of pitfalls is that we tend to believe in monolithic concepts, and that moral behavior of what is good or bad is fixed. Yet, we can witness from wall paintings, statutes and ancient writings, that moral concepts change with the times. We have endured thousands of years of trial and tribulations; only by investigating not by believing, can we humans reach rational conclusion from rational premises. We should investigate and not guide our actions by ideological morality, regardless of its origins.

3

WHO IS USING RECREATIONAL DRUGS?

"[Drug] companies will soon rule the world if we let them believe we are happy, functional society so long as all the women are on Prozac, all children on Ritalin, and all men on Viagra."

Terri Guillements

According to L.M. Vance, there were 1,702,537 drug arrests in 2009 in the USA. Almost half of these arrests were for possession of narcotics (marijuana). Would these (851,269) people have a criminal record for the rest of their lives? So, who are these arrested persons? Could one or more be your or my children? Although I am neither a drinker nor a drug user, I have members of my family who are both. What about your family? Do you know a family who uses drugs? Do you have a neighbour whose teenager is using drugs?

Pernicious addictions are a serious problem in every society for the majority of people who are "hooked." Addiction has many context in which to describe a psychological obsession or compulsion, as in gambling, video games, pornography, tele-vision and so on. Addiction can also be a physical dependency or neurobiological disorder as in alcoholism, nicotine addiction, compulsive overeating or impaired control over the use of licit or illicit drugs. This is a very widespread conviction shared by a number of psychologists, anthropologists, social thinkers and medical experts who tend to look deeper into this problem. The habit becomes a problem when it transforms itself into an addiction. Addiction is a problem only for the individual, not for society. For instance, if a person is suffering from alcoholism or drug addiction to prescribed pain killers or diet drugs, it causes harm only to him/her and not to other persons. However, no one person is "an island unto himself". The addiction touches other persons lives and interests, family, children, relatives, co-workers, friends and so on. Addictions are a real problem if we recognized the fact that it happens very often in many families. It also affects the whole society and reduces the overall productive efficiency. We should admit that the problem of addiction is a psychological and physiological disease that cannot be ignored.

Some addictions, such as smoking, bring health complications to the smoker, but it is not as harmful to others. If a person is smoking, it does not prevent him/her from raising his/her children, loving a partner, earning money, and being a good parent. The problem of smoking, or any other addiction, is closely connected with the issue of civil rights. Any law and rule that infringes on the smoker's lifestyle, violates his/her right to possess a drug (product) that can be harmful to himself, and to follow a life choice that most of us would not follow. Most of us hate the terrible smell of cigarette smoke. But if a person does not care, or wants to die prematurely, the rest of us can only try to educate the smoker to the apparent dangers of smoking. His/her addiction is a recreational use of cigarettes. A possible lung-related disease, the result of smoking, is a *medical problem,* not a criminal offence.

Alcoholism is a chronic disease characterized by the habitual addictive consumption of alcohol. Alcoholism is to a degree an interference with physical or mental health and normal family or work behavior. Alcoholism is both a physical and a psychological addiction. It effects the central nervous system by reducing anxiety, inhibition and feelings of guilt. It lowers alertness and impairs perception and judgment . Chronic alcoholism damages the brain, liver, heart and other organs. Treatment for alcoholism is performed by medical professionals with special training and requires a process of detoxification.

There are many myths and misconceptions about drug addiction. What causes a person to go from drug user to drug addict? Our society, in general, believes that drug use and drug addiction are strictly personal or social problems. Most of us who believe in this myth are victims of long "moralising" righteous propaganda of the temperance movement in various media communities. It tends to characterize parents, teenagers, older persons, artists and "free-thinkers" who take drugs as morally weak or as having criminal tendencies. They regard drug addiction as a criminal behavior rather than similar to an alcoholic behavior.

These misconceptions have stereotyped the persons with drug-related problems as well as their families and are judgemental towards the health care professionals who work with them. It is difficult for people who feel righteous to recognize that drug abuse and addiction comprise a public health problem that has wide-ranging social consequences. Addiction to licit or illicit drugs begins when a person makes a conscientious choice to use drugs that are potentially addictive for health or recreational reasons. Persons who are addicted to prescriptive or non-prescriptive drugs suffer from a compulsive drug craving. Medical treatment is necessary to end this compulsive behavior. Drug abuse has maimed, traumatized or displaced countless numbers of people. The social consequences are that drug use and abuse has remained embedded in our society and in the way we live.

WHY TEENAGERS USE DRUGS

Many teens try tobacco, alcohol or drugs. They try these "forbidden fruits" for many reasons. One of the reasons is peer pressure, where a teen wants to fit-in with friends or certain groups. They may also take drugs such as marijuana, because they like the way it makes them feel. Under current laws, possession of drugs for personal use is illegal. Does this illegality transform the social standing of the otherwise law-abiding teenagers into criminals? One possible answer may lie in the following point: in 1967, Canadian Prime Minister Pierre Eliot Trudeau declared his support for the decriminalization of abortion and homosexuality by stating *"There is no place for the state in the bedrooms of the nation."* Is the legal lifestyle of sexual orientation any different from the lifestyle of recreational drug use? My point is this: for a crime to be committed it must be against another person or property. Our teenagers, sons and daughters who are high school, college or university students are not committing a crime against the well-being of another person.

PERSONS SUFFERING FROM POST-TRAUMATIC STRESS DISORDER

Many societies have used, and still use, legitimate medical drugs that are under prohibition. For example, a legitimate medical use of an illegal drug is the use of MDMA. This illegal drug is administrated for cognitive enhancement to people with Parkinson's Disease, to people who have been raped, and to soldiers returning from war and suffering from PTSD. It is a synthetic, psychoactive drug, a chemical stimulant meth-amphetamine, and a hallucinogen mescaline. For the illegal recreational user, MDMA produces feelings of increased energy, euphoria and emotional warmth. It can produce distortions in time perception and tactile experiences. It is also addictive if taken in increased unauthorized doses. It should be noted that it is a drug experience that is similar to marijuana, cocaine, ketamine and other legal or illegal euphoric substances. One of these, marijuana, is an illegal drug (in most countries) that can be used medicinally for AIDS patients, chemotherapy and persons who suffer from nausea, cannabis increases relief.

MARGINALIZED PEOPLE

They are the sex workers, drug users, small time dope traffickers, homeless and teen runaways who reside in the inner cities or "skid-rows." These are people whose lives have become too difficult to cope with or who have made the wrong choices during their lifetimes. No one can ever know each person's personal history. A large number of them may suffer from some kind of mental illness, due to past personal tragedies or current lifestyle. Lack of proper shelter, food, personal hygiene, contaminated drug paraphernalia, drug impurities, HIV, Hepatitis C and 24/7 dangerous surroundings tend to contribute to a constant feeling of anxiety paranoia and, at times, to death. It is very easy to forget that each individual was or still is someone's loved child or a "black sheep" family member.

In such a marginalized environment, one can closely witness the authorities' "militarized" approach to solving a medical and social problem. The so called "war on drugs" is so actively played out. Arrests, beatings, violation of human rights, and racial and ethnic profiling is a common sight. I call this "society's shame" zone. Collectively, we have decided to criminalize or suppress the problem rather than solving it by decriminalizing the possession of drugs for personal use. The prohibition of heroin and crack cocaine often leads to fatalities, muggings, burglaries, use of infected needles, trafficking and unsafe prostitution. More on this later.

RECREATIONAL DRUG USERS

This is a broad classification term that includes police, judges, politicians, teachers, white collar workers, financiers, "weekend-warriors," the young and up-coming professionals. In such a clarification, I do not insert a moral or hypocritical innuendo regarding these "up-standing" citizens who are included in the above list of recreational drug users. It is a common sight to listen to and watch public entertainers and sports figures openly admit to their own recreational use of drugs, their addiction, their drug rehabilitation and so on. Mostly, these are the people who can effort to pay for their afford casual drug use and/or their drug addiction. They are often included in the new 'entertainment' of reality shows. Drug traffickers who serve the upper-class recreational drug users are part of the same social circle and "artistic environment." They are drug trafficking in order to pay for their own addictive habits and to earn the kind of money that would permit them to maintain themselves in such an exclusive environment. Therefore, as a rule, neither the recreational drug user nor the drug trafficker need be concerned with the status of decriminalization or the illegal sale of drugs. At this social level, money, not human misery, is the common denominator between buyer and seller of recreational drugs. Even so, the uncontrolled consumption of both licit and illicit drugs can give rise to depression, hallucinations, convulsions and sensations of excruciating pain or burning, known in the Middle Ages as St. Anthony's fire. The only possible common denominator between the upper-class recreational drug abuser and the rest is that one or both may become a statistic of those who suffer from:

- ❖ Tobacco which kills about   400,000 per year
- ❖ Alcoholism which kills about   80,000 per year
- ❖ Cocaine which kills about   2,500 per year
- ❖ Heroin which kills about   2,000 per year
- ❖ Aspirin which kills about   2,000 per year, and
- ❖ Marijuana which kills   0 per year

MENTAL PATIENTS

Several legal dilemmas are created by the prohibition of heroin, morphine, GHB and MDMA, which are illegal to possess, yet are inherently present in all humans as a result of the endogenous synthesis. Since the legal definition of illegal "possession" of drugs includes having the drug present in the patient's blood in any concentration, mental residents that are administered these drugs are technically in possession of multiple illegal drugs. Marijuana is an example of a mainly illegal drug that is used medicinally. AIDS patients control their nausea by using cannabis. Mental diseases such as depression, paranoia and psychosis may vary substantially in the treatment applied using prohibited drugs. Psychiatric therapy uses LSD, mescaline, phencyclidine & analogs, psilocybin, and amphetamine variants.

4

AMERICAN THEOCRACY AND PROHIBITION ALCOHOL & DRUGS

"[Religion is] a system of wishful illusions with a disavowal of reality, such as we find nowhere else but in a state of blisful hallucinatory confusion. Religion's eleventh commandment *"Thou shall not question."*

Sigmund Freud (The Future of an Illusion)

The influence of religion on ancient societies was obvious. However, it is also obvious in modern societies. In ancient Greek and Roman societies, religion, morals, and law were indistinguishable from one another. On the basis of this model, we should expect that in Egyptian and Israeli regions different arbitrary beliefs were handed down, to be believed with the same conviction as ideal traditional wisdom. Such traditional religious beliefs were also passed on to the newest religious cult, Christianity and much later, to Islam. For example, you can find in the First Commandment a religious command, *"God spake those words and said, I am Lord thy God."* We should also expect that taboos, superstitions and other non-factual beliefs evolved regionally and changed over generations–either by random drift or by some sort of acceptance selected from a diversity of traditions and worldviews.

Based on arbitrary beliefs that were handed down, every Christian can now claim to have the power to read God's mind which is instructing him/her to take a given action. This claim underlies the ability for one to have direct communication with God's demands or wishes. It is a ancient claim, which was uttered by temple priests, missionaries, religious fanatics and cultist leaders of minorities. While this power to communicate with God was once the exclusive prerogative of the few individuals, nowdays anyone can make the same claim. The key-word to connect with an imaginary entity lies in the utterance of certain 'magical' terms: "I am doing God's work…" or "God wants me to…" or "God sent me to…". Such magical words form a *"bridge-link"* between an imaginary entity and a believer's illusional claims. This bridge connection is similar to popular stories such as *"Sinbad and the Forty Thieves"*, where uttering the magical word *"abracadabra"* served as the key to open communication with an invisible entity. Many religious people call their Bible the "Good Book" that teaches them about good and bad, moral and immoral acts. Most believers find it hard to believe how, without following the Bible, one can be good, or even want to be good. This is a fundamental schism that drives these same religious people to extremes of hatred against those "others" who do not behave in a homogenous way. This schism is more apparent in the area of moral considerations. Religious expectations of chosen behaviour lie hidden behind religious attitudes towards other topics that have no real connection to morality. For example, uttering the magic words "God opposes drinking" forms a *bridge link* to prohibition on drinking. The same magic words can call for support to "doing God's work" as a *bridge-link* to imposing any sort of restriction on public behaviour. In the case of drinking, temperance advocates are doing God's work, not their work, for after all it is God who opposes drinking. Bridge-links to imaginary entities permit religious people to connect issues that are confined within their own imagination of what constitutes good or bad. The news about a group of Americans who went to Haiti in 2010 and attempted to remove 32 children from Haiti without permission is a case of a *bridge-link*. They claimed that "God sent us" to take those children away from their villages, even though the Haitian authorities told them ahead of time not to. Of course, they could not produce a factual written or spoken order from God, showing that they were doing his work. In short, *bridge-links* are ideas or words that are used to connect a *literal* with a *metaphorical* concept.

The basic nature of every cult or religious organization is for member obedience to its rules, customs, traditions or taboos. Within this structure, men, women and especially children, are numbered into thousands of innocent, well-meaning and eager persons. There are also others who are hell-bent on changing the world in accordance to their beliefs. Non-fundamentalist, sensible people may abstain from doing that. But I can confirm that the dividing line between fundamentalists and non-fundamentalists can be obscured. The problem with such obscurance is that no one would teach their children, from their early years, that questioning every belief, including their own faith, is a virtue. Unquestionable faith leads to the dark side of absolutism. In my book *Prisoners of Our Ideals* I show how such absolutism nearly always results from strong religious faith which constitutes a major reason to suggest that theocratic morality is a non-humanist morality. American theocracy rules the minds of a great number of people, mostly against something that believers must enforce upon others. That "something" has little to do with faith, and much to do with inspired theocratic cultural control over society. Such cultural control is based on directing believers to fear "something" and then sell it to them, so that they will fight against it in the name of "God's work." More than any other species, we have learned to obey whatever our grown-ups tell us–our parents, tribal elders, our 'betters' or church leaders–without question. Soldiers are drilled to become like automatons, and this characteristic is also shared by "God's soldiers". In the 1850's they were given, in their own specific language, the order to rid society of all social ills, starting with drinking and opium smoking. But above all, religious advocates of temperance were propagating a belief that morality consists in obeying the rules of the church. This is a theistic moral absolutism which binds all believers to the absolutes of right and wrong, without regard to the consequences of their righteousness. True enough, moral absolutism does not derive from religion alone. But a frenzy of absolute patriotism, as in "God and country," are an unbeatable team used by temperance advocates to fight the war on drugs in Latin America and around the world

Temperance reasoning against drugs/alcohol is used to influence the political decision to go to war on drugs. Once the war commences, it is held to be an absolute virtue. In fact, it is hard to get much more moralist-absolute than *"The wine is from God, but the drunkard is from the Devil"*. Once absolute morality takes over with *"God's force and power,"* a temperance believer's thoughts do not allow him/her to exerciseself-restraint. Doing "God's work", is the preferred reference of absolute morality which is interpreted as having an authority far beyond anyone or anything else. Indeed, adherents of cults and organized religious leaders show little curiosity about the roots of their temperance moral absolutism. Contemporary temperance advocates who claim to derive their morals from the Bible should take closer a look at the "Holy Book" and discover the many atrocities committed against humanity, in the name of absolute morality. They themselves, on reflection, should agree that cultural crimes against humanity should not be committed in the name of absolute rules of living.

Rational thinkers more pragmatically hold that the morality of an action should be judged by its actual or potential consequences. Absolute moralists, either religious or not, are short-sighted when imposing their rules of how to live. Admittedly, religious moral absolutism is very much alive today. It rules the dysfunctional minds of a great number of Americans, including the fundamentalists in powerful positions of setting public policy. Americans and the Muslim world are considered to be the most religious people on earth, although for different reasons. America was settled by revolutionaries with new ideas, and by political reactionaries with Protestant religious ethics. The former were overshadowed by the latter. The reactionaries were reacting against the Old World's political settings. They immigrated to the New World in order to establish a political utopian society based on their religiosity. European Puritans and others of the "Protestant work ethic" were ideological advocates of a strict absolute morality, guided by rules of biblical theocracy. One of the fiercest penalties was levied for deviating from prescribed theocratic rules of moral living. Any deviation from those rules could lead to the expulsion of the individual from the cult or church. In time, this created a culture of intolerance that risks going too far: where will it end now? In thinking like an automaton and prescribing behaviour for all? Is this an almost exact mirror image of totalitarianism, so willingly supported by millions of dysfunctional people in other parts of the world? Such reactionary ideology was passed on to the temperance from one generation to the next, without ever knowing the origins of thoughts and actions.

The temperance ideology is a by-product of religious intolerance, of imposing restrictions and punishments, and of propaganda rather than education. In the first case, temperance attempts to restrict alcohol and drug use by advocating punishment for those who are unwilling to obey by those restrictions. The relationship between restriction and punishment is present in the whole Biblical doctrine. For instance, Christianity restricts working on Sunday, for the Seventh Day Adventist it is Saturday, for Muslims it is Friday etc. Other restrictions fall under their definitions of *blasphemy*, *apostasy* or restrictions between a man and a woman. Moral contact consists of multiple restrictions that must be obeyed. Any deviation or violation of those moral rules will result in punitive measures. Punishment against offenders of moral rules is inevitable, whether here on earth or by the sky-God. In the second case, imposing obedience to moral rules is done through a cruel or sophisticated form of propaganda. Propaganda is distinct from education. The former includes the sin of disobedience, lies, distortions, fear or threats of potential punishment. Education is about questioning, investigating, experimenting, analysing trials and errors, and discovering a humane rule of behaviour that does not harm others.

As I said above, the ideology of temperance is a by-product of religious intolerance. Temperance is about restricting a behaviour under the threat of punishment. It has a typical reactionary religious characteristic that includes propaganda, restrictions, and punishment. Temperance is not a pro-active educational movement. Its propaganda contains cruel forms of religious delusions, as well as sophisticated distortions of reactionary indoctrination. What is actually wrong with religious temperance? Does it really do so much harm that we should actively oppose it? Isn't religious temperance just harmless nonsense? I might retort with political incorrectness, but my stand is limited to using rational words. I am not going to call them insulting names just because of a rational disagreement with them.

The first reported temperance organization in America, which promulgated a moral restriction from alcohol, was formed in New England in 1808. Most members of temperance groups considered temperance to be a religious issue because they felt compelled to serve God. Members of temperance, including their leaders, were simultaneously committed members of a variety of religious groups, such as Congregationalist, Baptist, Mormon, Roman Catholic, Presbyterians, Seventh Day Adventists, and others. Much later, the infamous Ku Klux Klan also joined the temperance movement. Members of temperance groups claimed the imposition of temperance due to their God. Religion was the effective weapon for temperance advocates. Their typical pledge was somewhat hypocritical, as in *"We pledge to abstain from all intoxicating liquors except for...religious ordinance"*.

During the early 1850's, many religious advocates of various denominations became convinced that the majority of rural men were living in an immoral manner. They looked around at the existing dreadful social environment with its poverty, ignorance, sicknesses, unemployment, lack of education and raising crime. Because of these conditions, they feared that God would no longer bless America. Solving these social ills, therefore, was a question of adopting the right moral structure. In other words, they were looking inwards instead of outwards to solve problems that existed outside of themselves.

Fear against the "other", such as against those who were "immoral", "ungodly", or "unscrupulous" frontier men is a primary religious irrationality. Mixing fear, God, absolute morality and patriotism, these religious fundamentalists reacted towards existing social ills as being a threat to America's political order. Morality was a lot easier to sell than correcting real social and economic inequalities amongst people. They reacted in the same manner as their reactionary counterparts in the 1840's in Europe, who also viewed social ills as a problem of morality, and then immigrated to America. Reactionary religious absolutism persuaded them of the need to make the ungodly believe, because America needed virtuous citizens who did not engage in immoral acts, such as drinking, hanging around "drinking-holes" (taverns) and being rowdy. In time, however, their reactionary strategy changed from moral persuasion to political tactics. If abstinence from drinking could not be achieved by religious moral rules, then legal restriction was the alternative. Alcohol drinking thus became their rally point of condemnation. Causes for all other social ills were attributed to alcohol consumption.

Religious leaders in small-town America were missionaries whose wives had no choice but to follow their husbands to the frontier. Some missionaries, like of the Moravian Church, were sent to convert the Indians to Christianity. Small-town Americans lived in primitive conditions until their land could be cleared, become productive and provide employment. Settlers also had to deal with annoying rowdy transients who contributed very little to the harmony of the town. Nearly all small towns provided little social interaction other than for men to go to the taverns and for women to gather in the churches. Because men were away from home for long hours, working in the fields, hunting or spending time in the local bars, their wives were left behind with no adult companionship. There are numerous accounts of loneliness, depression and even occasional suicides. Most of the men followed their biblical traditions of opposing women from having a life outside of the home. Women were to nurture their husbands and to raise virtuous children so that the nation could become a republican utopia. This concept was advocated by preachers and their wives in Sunday sermons and gatherings whose main attendance were women. This concept was known as the Republican Motherhood. Sunday or afternoon sermons intentionally or un-intentionally focused on problems of immorality in the community. Men's drinking and related domestic problems were among the immoral acts that most women listening to sermons on this issue tended to agree with. Others who also tended to agree with the issue of drinking included the local farmers and businessmen who could not always depend on the local help. They needed a disciplined and sober workforce. Most women were focused on convincing their husbands, fathers, sons and brothers to reduce their consumption of alcohol, although these women would not have objected to complete abstinen

As the issue of men's drinking took its own momentum, it became a self-perpetuating organism. In church sermons, women prayed for the souls of their drinking men folk and of the bar patrons. When all was said and done, some women were encouraged by the preacher's sermons, and attempted to block the entrances of local liquor stores and bars that sold alcoholic drinks. These acts of public display were done spontaneously. This is the typical beginning of every social and apolitical movement that lacks a strict organizational structure. It was also chance for local and national political opportunists to capitalise on group hysteria by inserting their own agenda onto the group's social momentum. Anyone who was someone jumped on the bandwagon of the informal temperance group action, using an underlying religiosity to rid "the root of all evil"while promoting their own agenda. Many religious leaders initiated their own style of morality which was needed for building a Christian nation. Women's frustration with futile attempts of changing their men's drinking habits was viewed as a means of achieving a political base and support for other issues. Local and national entrepreneurs, who needed a steadily available work force, saw women as a vehicle to get men to stop drinking. Women began to form temperance groups that were tragically doomed due to their idealistic sense of social entrapment. Their idealism concerned their expectations about their role as women in the 19th century patriarchal society. They could not reconcile the reality of their middle-class lives with their idealized vision of what they thought life should be. They were victimized by their idealized perspective on reality. Putting their own misguided idealism and their religious faith in the hands of the theocratic clergymen sealed their fate. Theocratic delusions convinced them that it was not the dreadful inequalities of social conditions that suppressed their liberation, but their husbands' immoral acts, which turned out to be a deliberately induced illusion. Under such an illusion, women could never have fully achieved the religious vision of idealized love at home.

Was the issue of drinking such an overwhelming habit that it turned into a morality cause and a political bandwagon for many? In colonial America and during the 1850's, alcoholic beverages–brewed, fermented or distilled–were an important part of the daily diet. Social attitudes viewed homemade liquor as "the good creature of God". All social groups (including preachers who drank "medicinal-alcohol") drank socially. Some drank for stress relief. Most people did not have a history of daily heavy drinking. For them, alcohol drinking became an "issue" when their wives brought it to their attention. Women were persuaded by the attraction of the belief that *drinking-is-a-problem,* which was associated with the general outcry against drunkards (the term for alcoholics).

Most temperance groups or formal organizations were dominated by ministers who made a considerable effort to create a *bridge-link* between their religion and temperance aspirations. They created and encouraged the public delusion of a non-existent epidemic of alcoholism, on the level with the "black death", swine flu or the cholera epidemic. They fed the public, especially the women worshipers, with a fear-mongering propaganda about the evils of alcohol. During sermons, ministers reminded men of their responsibilities to their wives, of liberating themselves from *King Alcohol* and from the terrible fate of eternal damnation, and renewed the prospect of heavenly salvation. They had long realized that their usual call to repentance from sins carried no punch. But having women turn towards the non-issue of men's drinking became a much more personal and subjective affair. To induce the public's delusions with more realistic flavour, ministers adopted the biblical expression of *parables,* describing to their congregation their own "experience" with alcoholism, to provide a basic agenda of rules for moral behaviour. They encouraged a public frenzy focused on the singular theme of drinking alcohol, which was also associated with murder, rape, immorality, cholera, fever, and epilepsy. The public, in their frustration and sense of helplessness about their own living conditions and their lack of understanding of the causes of social ills, found an expressive, simplistic panacea to all that was wrong with the world. If they could only abolish alcohol drinking, all would be well. Ministers and political opportunists encouraged and focused the public's attention on that singular theme of alcohol drinking as if drinking alcohol was all that men were doing day-in and day-out. Much credit should be given to the religious leaders who appreciated the power that religious delusions had over women and the public in general. Donations kept increasing, and so were the members of their congregations. All felt that they were on the road to godly salvation.

As the temperance movement was spreading across the country, and as public frenzy kept fermenting, the direction of it changed from moral indoctrination to legalistic and political action. Morality was enforced upon group members by enacting by-laws of moral conduct. Although each temperance group had its own variation of rules of moral conduct, the following is from the Allenton Sober Society of 1805.

1) *Any member taking a bottle or glass through deception to make a pretence of drink, although they do not drink, shall pay the sum of 25 cents.*

2) *Any member having been disowned must pay $ 1.00 for re-instatement.*

3) Be it further enacted, that if any member takes the use of God's name in vain [blasphemy] or swear in manner during the time the Society are sitting, is to pay the sum of six cents for every offence.

In predominantly "Bible-Belt" counties, religious moralists beliefs were often the catalysts for temperance. Though secular advocates began to participate and organize groups whose aims included religious affiliates, they're prominent examples of movements that initiated the beginnings of feminism and religious morality. The most prominent supporters of temperance have been women, who were opposed to domestic violence, who supported a larger share of matrimonial property, voting rights etc. Because the concept of temperance had become so prominent in the public's view, most groups with diversified goals preferred to function under the social umbrella of temperance. Semi-temperance movements were mainly movements of socialism, social democracy, Christian democracy, nationalism and fascism, which had also been strongly connected to the cause of women's rights and alcohol abstinence. Formal domestic controls in the home and in communities in America were equated with the lack of women's freedom in other forms of social infractions. While women began by advocating temperance in the use of alcohol, the movement now insisted that other women's issues should become major issues in every political campaign from the national, state and local level down to those for school board members. Religious temperance rules of morality had to be legislated by politicising men's "drinking problem".

The Civil War (1861-1865) interrupted the temperance movement, but not its underlying momentum. After the war, veterans returned home to be reminded of the "issue" of their "drinking problem". On this basis, the *Women's Christian Temperance Union* was founded to promote not just the moderation of drinking but rather total prohibition. The WCTU was founded and organized by Mary Hunt, whose efforts established the *Department of Scientific Instruction in Schools and Colleges.* This gave a chance for political opportunists to build up a national compulsory *Scientific Temperance Instruction Movement* to be included in school curriculum. Because of the correlation between alcoholism and domestic violence, the temperance movement existed alongside various women's rights, new political ideologies, and often the same participants were also involved in all of the above. Many former abolitionists joined the temperance movement and it was also strongly supported by the second Ku Klux Klan, which formed the military side of prohibition enforcement. For the following decades until the end of 1800's, prohibition aspirations were touted as the most advocated magical solution to America's problems of poverty, crime, violence, and other social ills. At the beginning of the 20th century, all of the temperance organizations stressed political results. Hence, the people who were engaging in the crusade against alcohol were zealous propagandists who adopted the politics of prohibition, rather than the platform of religious morality. Large financial donations, earnings from printed books and pamphlets, earnings from folk-art painting depicting moralist scenes of prohibition and political influence, pulled the prohibition movement more and more away from its religious origins. The old temperance movement was now hijacked and used as a right-wing political force i.e. the Prohibition Party and others. Propaganda was in full political force to influence, manipulate and exploit the naiveté and ignorance which was promoted by religious delusions. No political or community figure had attempted to investigate the consequences of enforcing prohibition. Prohibition was seen as a beginning and an end unto itself, within the confines and isolation of religious delusion and the polarization of morality. The WCTU began a crusade to shut down working-class saloons and middle class bars, and to advocate total abolition rather than merely temperance. Religious morality was sidestepped–maintained only for public consumption–and the main goal was to lobby major political parties for total abolition. By 1912, local prohibition laws were passed making most of the South "Bible

Belt" legally dry. The legal definition of "dry" meant very little to the moonshine bootleggers who filled the gap in the market and replaced the legal sales of alcohol. What was about to become a national crime industry was ignored due to the legal "accomplishments" of prohibition advocates. They were blinded by their 100 or more years of believing in their own delusions. They were not willing to see the potential human tragedy that was about to begin by the appearance of gangsterism and the actual rise of alcohol consumption. By 1917, the WCTU, rich with donations and political influence, pushed for the termination of industrial alcohol distilling, the selling of liquor near military bases, or the serving liquor to servicemen in uniform. Saloons, a social heaven for man, were viewed by many, especially women, as a place of debauchery and evil. Women's ever-present ambition, to transform men after their own image, to create their ideal man, a domesticated creature with no vices or bad habits, was about to be tested by reality—not by their wishful thinking. In the same year, prohibition was implemented through thirty-three (33) state legislatures. By 1918, the 18th Amendment to the US Constitution had been proposed to establish the Volstead Act— called National Prohibition—which was ratified on January 16, 1919. It went into effect one year later, on January 16, 1920, prohibiting the manufacturing, sale and transportation of alcoholic spirits.

For more than 120 years, white middle-class religious moralists felt that America needed to restore a strong moral foundation, which would be the overall magical solution to poverty (associated with immigrants), crime (associated with the working class), and corruption (associated with the rich). Poverty, crime and immoral acts were associated with the use of alcohol (at any level of consumption). Alcohol became the anti-Christ evil, King Alcohol, which prevented the bringing about of a Christian morality. Economics and the just distribution of labour-created wealth was placed secondary to a virtuous and moral nation. The Reverent Henry Ward Beecher was quoted in Harper's Weekly, May 8, 1886, summarising the ignorance to the real causes of desperation, personal sense of failure etc.

"I do not say a dollar a day is enough to support a working man, but its enough to support a man [as if there is a distinction between a working man and a man]. *Not enough to support a man and five children if a man insists on smoking and drinking beer."*

Such twisted logic is typical of self-satisfied clergymen whose daily cost of living is guaranteed by people's donations and institutional investments.

The constitutional prohibition of alcohol, from 1920 to 1933, was one of the most idiotic social experiments in America, next to the prohibition of drugs enacted by the Harrison Act of 1914. Since the early 20th century, misguided aspirations waxed and waned and produced numerous state prohibitions. Most of the prohibitions that persisted were widely ineffective. The forces behind them followed closely the biblical instructions of rules for moral conduct. They made sure that the "sinners" who consumed alcohol obeyed religious morality or were punished. Since their biblical books do not contain an educational instructional process, but rather acts of obedience and punishment, ministers followed a strict dogmatic order. Amid the hysterical atmosphere created by the long lasting prohibition movement, support for it was increased by the mass propaganda of the Hearst media empire, known to create events/conditions in order to generate publicity. Mass media propaganda reinforced a *herd-mentality* for the majority of prohibitionists who weren't bothered by the lack of empirical evidence for mass alcoholism. Their actions were compartmentalised from any alternative rational solutions, i.e. education instead of obedience, medical-treatment instead of prison punishment. Along with Protestant religious groups, who believed in the literal interpretation of the Bible and the rules of moral conduct, they represented a subculture of influence in local women's temperance movements. The size of the theocratic subculture was an important factor in politicizing prohibition; its influence was most notable within the public policy body of the state legislatures. Support of strict liquor prohibition reflected a set of regulations on morality stemming from Protestantism's Puritan inheritance, with its emphasis on obedience, hard work and wealth growth, and from Protestant aspirations to instil a religious faith based on piety and the acceptance of asceticism (self-denial). Puritan and Calvinist pietistic propagation found drinking, dancing, gambling, love, happiness, romance, and pre-marital sex, as "forbidden fruit" activities that brought down God's wrath on man and his society. Descriptive analysis of the language used in the enactment of liquor and drug prohibitions suggest that the various Protestant religious denominations were responsible, either directly or indirectly in working under women's groups–Anti-Saloon League, Women's Christian Temperance Union–for the passage of prohibitive laws.

Prohibition is a negative social condition with equally predictable negative consequences. It can be imposed on a single product, a set of products, or as a law of *"blanket-prohibition"*. Prohibition of a single product can be drugs, alcohol or the series of products itemized in the *Chronology* section of this book. In turn, a "blanket prohibition" can be imposed as, for example, a) a freeze on overall government job hiring, b) a freeze on importing products from certain countries, due to health reasons, c) a prohibition on the importation of non-essential products, and d) a prohibition on foreign products that are unfairly competing against local producers etc. Prohibitive laws are the "power-arm" of every government, and are continually enforced against one or another product or service. Prohibition creates an opportunity for by-passing itself, through loop-holes that are inherent in every legal prohibition. Federal, state and local legislators are familiar with loop-holes and work diligently to avoid them by creating air-tight legislations. Beyond the legal definition of loop-holes, however, there are social forces where the legal application of prohibition does not apply. These are the consequences which result in the illegal opportunities to counter-act prohibition. In other words, legally operated corporations are using legal loop-holes to by-pass prohibition, while the illegal enterprises simple violate all legal definitions and descriptions of prohibition.

In the case of Alcohol Prohibition, it provided opportunities for illegal enterprises to counter-act liquor prohibition. Those illegal enterprises are called bootlegging, liquor smuggling, liquor contraband etc. In the case of Drug Prohibition (as in the Harrison Act of 1914), the illegal enterprises that counter-act drug prohibition are known as drug traffickers who manufacture, transport and sell illegal drugs. In the case of blanket prohibition, let's say, prohibition of non-essential foreign products, there exist legal "loop-holes" upon which legal enterprises challenge the strict legal definition of 'non-essential-products'. When imported products are defined by loop-hole as being essential, their importation would be granted. Otherwise, blanket prohibition consequences create opportunities for illegal enterprises to smuggle, by means of contraband, products that can be sold for large profits. Also, there is the underground production of imitation non-essential products which are manufactured to meet the local demands for those products. Because those products are manufactured by unregulated enterprises, quality is not up to normal standards. During the Alcohol Prohibition of 1920-1933, illegal alcohol for human consumption was of poor quality and at times poisonous. No wonder that liver diseases and blood poisoning was a common health problem during alcohol prohibition. This is also true today with the unhygienic production of cocaine and other illegal drugs. The purity of the illegal drugs are "cut" with chemicals to increase the volume, and thus increase the drug dealers profits. The quality and origins of the "cutting" agents are not known and cannot be verified.

From 1914 to 1920, prohibition laws against drugs and alcohol in the US emerged due to theocratic societies devoted to imposing public virtue and moral restrictions on their fellow Americans. They lobbied local, state and federal legislators for additional laws prohibiting behaviour they considered to be un-Christian, notably against gambling, sex workers, alcohol consumption and the use of non-prescription recreational drugs. Theocratic demands for the total legal suppression of un-Christian behaviour increased in intensity towards the end of 1920, mostly justified by a threat to Protestant morality and women's desire for man's ideal behaviour at home. By the end of 1920, both Protestant-led and woman's moral groups could claim a victory in having their aspirations become official state and federal laws. The same moral crusaders exploited American racism and xenophobia to support and spread their prohibition propaganda. For example, the First World War spread anti-immigrant anti-German, anti-Irish, and anti-Chinese propaganda because of their association with opium. The idea was propagated that drugs encouraged sexual promiscuity between the races which threatened the purity of the white race. Opium dens from New York to San Francisco were found to be humiliating signs of having white women and Chinese men sharing a "high" under the effects of the opium. Racist prejudice against American Blacks was fuelled by arguments seeking to suppress the once legally purchased and free use of cocaine. Claiming that cocaine made rapists of black men–or encouraged them to have sex with white women–was long a fundamentalist racial policy. Also, there was an underlying fear that cocaine helped black men achieve immense strength and astuteness under its influence. On the racial forefront, religious fundamentalist Dr Hamilton Wright ,author of the 1910 Report on the International Opium Commission, says that

"...this new vice, the cocaine vice, the most serious to be dealt with, has proven to be the creator of criminals and unusual

forms of violence, and it has been a potent incentive in driving the humble negroes all over the country to abnormal crimes.(Helmer,1975, p. 12)

During the 13 year period from 1920 to 1933, contended exaggerated claims, hysterical language, and racial stereotyping contended that half of the American population was effected by alcohol and drugs, which was the main cause of feeble mindedness and sexual perversion of white middle-class women. Christian fundamentalists of the Anti-Saloon League and the WCTU gathered crowds in churches and religious camp revival meetings, and continued to launch profitable careers from receiving a percentage of the donations. Simultaneously, commercial and industrial leaders were hoping that the Alcohol Prohibition would create a sober and docile workforce that would not be wasting wages in gambling, prostitution, drinking and taking drugs. They arrived into the twisted logical conclusion that if the workers were not spending money on wasteful activities, they were less likely to demand higher wages.

On the anti-drug front, the Harrison Narcotic Act's original intention was to organize the manufacturing and sales of drugs and related tax provisions. It was intended to provide federal internal revenue by imposing a special tax on enterprises or persons who produced, imported, manufactured, dealt in, dispensed, sold or distributed opium or coca leaves, their alkaloids and derivatives. It was also intended to place a control on the drug prescriptions given by the medical profession. Theocratic hold didn't limited itself to alcohol prohibition alone. Propagators of theocratic power were involved in every aspect of social life where it could impose its rules on public morality. For example, the Episcopal Bishop C. H. Brent convened a *Commission of Inquiry* on the subject of opiates. Along with the theistic-racist Dr Hamilton, mentioned above, both concluded that:

"...cocaine is often the direct incentive to the crime of rape by negroes of the South and other parts of the country" or *"...one of the most unfortunate phases of smoking opium in this country is the large number of women who have become involved and were living as common-law wives or cohabitating with Chinese in the Chinatowns of our various cities."*

The fact that a white woman could possibly have a relationship with an Oriental man was a nail driven into Puritanical sexual morality. Protestant moralists and career demagogues of the temperance movement were all out for strengthening alcohol and drug prohibition. Although the Harrison Narcotic Act of 1914 was not intended to be a prohibition law, these pro-prohibitionists were successful in distorting the intended purpose of the legislative Act. Occupying or controlling key positions within the Treasury Department, they began an intense campaign to exploit the ambiguity in the wording of the Act to outlaw opiates and other drugs totally. Motivated by their religiosity for total theocratic control of public morality, they even restricted doctors from practicing their occupational calling of treating drug addicts. Thousands of doctors were arrested, convicted and sentenced to penitentiaries for breaking the law that was not prohibitive in the first place. Doctors were prohibited from dispensing cocaine, heroin or morphine to drug addicts or as a way to reduce the pain of the terminally ill. Despite their professional medical opinion that these drugs were most effective in reducing pain, religious zealots made sure that medical practices didn't contradict theocratic impositions.

This was the beginning of drugs becoming a police problem rather than a medical problem. Alcoholism and drug addiction became a crime that is still in the legal books of the United States justice system. Thus, both Acts had immediately made problems of criminality and corruption far worse than it was prior to prohibition. Within a short time, both prohibitions' consequences were robberies and hijackings of drugs and alcohol. Within a few days following the Alcohol Prohibition, the first of many Treasury agents were arrested for liquor law corruption, and by the end of 1933 more than 15,000 agents were charged or dismissed for corruption. The two main features of drug and alcohol prohibition were the apparent negative consequences of the laws that overloaded the American criminal justice system and prisons.

There is an ancient Arabic saying, *"A camel can only see another camel's hump"* in reference to someone finding faults in others, while **not** seeing his/her own faults. We in North America are overly identifying Muslim theocratic authoritarian regimes in Iran, Pakistan, Afghanistan, Saudi Arabia or in Muslim theocratic organizations living amongst us. We see the theocratic "hump" in those countries and groups, but we do not see the sophisticated Christian theocratic hold that small and large religious organizations command over the rest of us. We are reacting to other countries' "hump" but we are blinded by our own theocratic society "hump". We are reacting to other nationalities' faults, but we are not acting on our own faults. Are we a nation of reactionaries? Are we so manipulated that we no longer see the theocratic hold of many legislators propagating as American ideals? Is this why we are compartmentalising the theocratic absolute morality of drug prohibition from its physical consequences of persecution and imprisonment of our fellow citizens? Have you ever asked yourself why, after 120 years of theocratic propaganda and tragic human misery, the "glory" of theocratic morality of Alcohol Prohibition lasted only 13 years? Can you see your own "hump"?

5

NATURE OF PROHIBITIONS

"Prohibitions only drive [addiction] behind doors and to dark places and does not cure it or even diminish it."

Mark Twain, May 28, 1867

To gradually crush some social acts, humans had to declare those acts "illegitimate" and their prohibitions justifiable. The creation of prohibitions is the fundamental basis of social control imposed on distinct groups of society. The system of prohibitions is based on the laws of the land. It evolves gradually to bring to the foreground, slowly but certainly, the imposition of a set of prohibitions. The prohibitor sets a multiplicity of laws to manage the human world, in a number of necessary historical stages.

SOCIAL TABOOS

One of the fundamental forms of prohibition on human behavior–which is embedded in social governance–is called a taboo. Its root lies in magico-religious bans the breaking of which entails a supernatural/theistic punishment. Christian, Jewish and Islamic taboos include gender behavior, food consumption, hygiene, marriage, sexual behavior, property rights and so on. The social system of the taboos can be considered as one of the most ancient rules which separated various human acts between "right" and "wrong", "good" and "evil", "permitted" and "prohibited".

RELIGIOUS MORALITY AND PROHIBITION

Mechanisms of the prohibition of human tendencies were born through religious morality which led to a written set of rules. Major religions imposed their morality to distinguish their notion between "good" and "evil". This began to include the basis of what current legislations and civil law, distinguishes between "legal" and "illegal" acts. A group of prohibitions which involved the taboos united the religious morality and the legislative laws to the point where both were obliging man to control more of his instincts and desires.

Throughout human history some religious taboos and moral prescriptions went out of use and disappeared because they were replaced by secular legislative laws. By the beginning of the 19th century, taboos, religious morality, and legal prohibitions more and more were redefined concepts–from legal or illegal into concepts of good or evil. The legal system of prohibition gradually gave up its function of regulating human tendencies of social behaviour. The evolution of the system of prohibitions required the work of religious moralists and similar minded legislators, judges and policemen. Indeed, an integral part of the system of prohibition is made up of persons who break the civil code, the religious moral code or the code of religious ethics. They break the main religious moral, ethical or civil rules of society by satisfying their personal tendencies which stand opposite to prohibitions. Obviously, in partisan ethics, what is favourable to one prohibitionist group is unfavourable to another group which is breaking religious moral taboos. Therefore, a person stays in opposition to religious ethics or morality while staying within the framework of the prohibition. It is a dialectical case of the unity of opposites.

TEMPERANCE MOVEMENT

The temperance movement is an ideological and political organisation of prohibitions. Its aim is to increase its influence and lobbying power in public policy matters regarding potentially prohibited products. It also promotes an aggressive enforcement of prohibition laws. Simultaneously, temperance organizations are attempting to eliminate any criticism or opposition to what they call society's purification from social ills. For the sake of clarity, temperance movements are not consumer protection organisations. They simply are against anyone using products that prohibitionists regard as unethical or immoral, according to their own definition of religious morality. These immoral or unethical products are liquor and drugs that are regarded as being recreational.

It should be noted that a temperance organization is not authorized by the federal government to intrude into people's personal habits of eating, drinking, dressing, smoking or using recreational drugs. Indeed, as an example, before the Harrison Narcotics Tax Act of 1914, there were no federal liquor and drug prohibition laws in the United States. Temperance movements have a specific political agenda that is disguised under biblical sermons and morality. Their singular aim is to influence and support political authorities that abide to a temperance political agenda. This is the primary reason why they were organized in the first place: to use their base power to influence the political system on their behalf. The argument from the standpoint of individual liberty and freedom from government or temperance intrusion into one's personal life is of no consequence. In short, temperance movements waxed and waned in the United States, New Zealand, Australia, the United Kingdom, Ireland, Canada and Sri Lanka as social movements against the recreational use of alcohol and drugs. They all pressured their governments to enact prohibition laws. From 1789, when the first temperance society was formed in Litchfield, Connecticut, to 1919 when the 18th Amendment was added to the US Constitution, temperance organizations finally achieved their goal: the prohibition of producing, distributing and selling of alcohol and drugs. From 1920 on, both prohibited products were prescribed in large quantities by physicians to their registered clients, as "medicinal-drugs".

PROHIBITION UNDER BLUE LAWS

Blue laws are a kind of state law, specifically found in the US, Israel and provinces of Canada. Blue laws are legally designed to enforce religious prohibitions, particularly the observance of Sunday as a day of worship and a prohibition on Sunday shopping. Blue law prohibitions typically target the sale of alcoholic beverages, groceries and drugs. Some Blue laws often prohibit shopping activities between certain hours due to religious principles. Methodist and Seventh Day Adventists observe their own prohibitions. In the US (2010) the following states enforce Blue laws of some degree on liquor and drugs: Arizona, Arkansas, Colorado, Connecticut, Georgia, Illinois, Indiana, Iowa, Louisiana, Massachusetts, Michigan, Minnesota, Mississippi, Missouri, New Jersey, New York, North Carolina, North Dakota, Ohio, Oklahoma, Oregon, Pennsylvania, South Carolina, Tennessee, Texas, Utah, Virginia, Washington, and West Virginia.

THE EFFECTS OF PROHIBITIONS: QUALITY OF DRUGS

The most direct effects of any kind of prohibitions are on the quality and price or supply and demand for the prohibited products. Often illegal drugs or alcohol (like moonshine) are manufactured in underground laboratories, where there is no care for hygiene. The products may be mixed or cut with other substances to increase supply, sale, potential profit or user addiction. Let's briefly look at the production of cocaine in the underground kitchens of Peru or Bolivia, South America, which I am familiar with.

Coca leaves sold in rural markets are a common sight in the Sierras and the jungles of Peru and Bolivia. The cultivation and distribution of coca leaf is a basic economic activity. The production of cocaine is one such economic activity.

Cocaine sulphate or pasta de coca is the intermediary stage between the coca leaf and the finished cocaine hydrochloride crystal. Coca leaves are submerged into a plastic pit with a solution of water and sulphuric acid (car battery acid solution). Out of this process a grey stuff is formed. This coca base is normally smoked by poor addicts in the slums. It is highly addictive and contains dangerous impurities in the way it is processed. The next stage of producing cocaine hydrochloride is much more complicated. In making pure cocaine the pasta de coca is submerged and washed in kerosene (a substance widely used to power aircraft jet engines). The mix is then highly chilled and the kerosene is removed. Gas crystals of crude cocaine are left at the bottom of the pit. These crystals are submerged and dissolved in methyl alcohol. These are once again re-crystallised and dissolved in sulphuric acid. Following additional processes these crystal are washed, oxidized and separated by using potassium permanganate, benzene, and sodium carbonate. This final product is pure cocaine. It contains dangerous by-products (impurities) and it is manufactured under un-hygienic conditions. The reason for this is simple: manufacturing cocaine is illegal and punishable severely by law. The illicit manufacturers are unqualified in chemistry, and are not bided by law to produce cocaine without impurities. Most workers in cocaine kitchens are users themselves, illiterate and hidden from the law. They care litle about hygiene, purifying procedures and clean water. Since they live and produce cocaine in the remote areas of the jungle, where water is needed to be carried by hand from some distance, washing and maintaining of bodily hygiene is difficuld. In short, water is recycled for both personal needs and cocaine production. Jungle parasites and animal feces are not removed before using water for mixing coca leaves in the initial state of the cocaine process. On the other hand, in the legal manufacturing process of cocaine, there are legal guidelines that outline the aspects of quality control. Governments around the world have legislated pharmaceutical companies to specific guidelines:

❖ Manufacturing processes must be validated to ensure consistency and compliance with specifications.

❖ Changes that have an impact on the quality of the drugs are validated as necessary.

❖ Operators must be trained to qualify in carrying out manufacturing procedures.

❖ Records must be kept during the manufacturing of cocaine to ensure that the quality and quantity of cocaine is as expected.

❖ Distribution methods of the drugs must minimize any risk to the quality.

❖ A system must be available for recalling any batch of drug for sale or supply.

These legal rules are followed during the production process.

DISTRIBUTION OF ILLICIT DRUGS

Often illegal drugs are purchased and distributed in the underground market. Prohibitions raise supply cost because the illicit market suppliers have to take extra precautions and face legal consequences for manufacturing, distributing and selling drugs. In distribution channels, there are many supplier between the manufacturing kitchens of drug cocaine and the purchaser/user on the street level. Let's follow a typical distribution of one kilo of "pure" cocaine en route to an underground market in the USA, Canada, Europe or Japan.

Supplier # 1, purchases one kilo of 100% pure cocaine that has been smuggled into the USA. Following a classical case of drug cutting (diluting), the rational for such cutting is greed–the supplier can quickly turn one kilo of 100% pure cocaine into two kilograms by mixing it with adulterant agents. Any white powder, including chalk, salt, flour, baking powder, novocaine or any chemical that is inexpensive and easy to obtain that mimics the physical characteristics of cocaine will do the job. Therefore, this supplier now has two kilograms of cocaine at 50% purity each. He simply has doubled his value by receiving twice the revenue.

Supplier # 2, has now purchased one kilo of adulterated cocaine at 50% purity. By mixing it with diluters of his choice, this would give the dealer two kilograms (of 25% strength drug each kilo). He now sells the two kilograms of 25% pure cocaine in small quantities to a street-level distributor. He thus also increases his money by receiving twice the revenue.

Supplier # 3 may or may not be a street-level distributor. He knows that the cocaine he just purchased is not pure. What he does not know is what kind of adulterants were used prior to his purchasing. At this level of cocaine distribution the purity can be as low 10-15% of the active drug with the other 85-90% diluted with safe or unsafe cutting agents. Impurities produced in the original manufacturing stage, and in the various steps in the distribution and improperly storing process, tend to endanger the health of the cocaine users.

LEGAL DRUG REGULATIONS & QUALITY CONTROL

In the western world, governments have regulated liquor and drug products. The focus of this regulation is simple; it is based on ensuring the quality and safety of liquor and drug consumption. From aspirin to whiskey, barbiturates to pain killers, heroin, cocaine or opiates in general, the necessity for government regulation lies in one of the most enduring problems. The historical fact in liquor or drug production has been the issue of cheap adulteration.

Adulteration means the cheapening of products through the addition of impurities or inferior ingredients. Historically, producers of liquor and drug products have attempted to alter their products in an effort to obtain higher profit margins from cheaper quality or increase their addictive strength. Case in point is the cigarette industry's experiments in Brazil to increase tobacco nicotine's addictive levels. It is known, for example, that water has been added to wine, inferior alcohol added to hard liquors and starch or plasma to drug ingredients. Thus, regulations governing what can or cannot be added to liquors or drugs, their official weights and measures, is standard practice today. This is because liquor and drug adulteration can pose both economic and health risks to people consuming poisoning contaminants. Given this environment, general liquor and drug regulations require producers to properly label their products to indicate whether mixtures or impurities are added. Hence, there is a growing perception that regulations for drug quality control is necessary. Such quality control simply does not exist in the illegal manufacturing and sale of cocaine.

PROHIBITION OF HEROIN/MORPHINE

In 1805, a German chemist, Frederich W.A. Serturner, successfully isolated and described morphine. Since its discovery, heroin/morphine has been legally used for medical/surgical cases as a painkiller and anaesthetic. Heroin, also known as diacetyl morphine is produced from the acetylating of morphine derived from opium poppies. Numerous processes and chemical means are used to purify the final product. Such final products have differences depending on the purity content and are marketed under a variety of names. However, the use of non-medical prescribed heroin/morphine is prohibited by law in most of the world's countries.

Illegal heroin opiate generally is smuggled into the United States and Europe from Colombia, Mexico, Southeast Asia and Afghanistan, which currently exports 94% of the world's heroin. Illicit heroin that reaches the street user ("for shooting up") is diluted at the production stage to a purity of 50%. The other 50% could be other opiate by-products of making heroin from opium. Additionally, most "hard" drugs on the street level are adulterated to some degree or other. The illegal drug dealer would attempt to find a chemical adulterant that would also be water-soluble and can be "cooked" in a spoon or silver-foil. If the dealer is unqualified in chemistry, the heroin may contain large quantities of contaminants including pyridine and acetic anhydride, which can be toxic. There have been a number of deaths reported due to "shooting up" heroin contaminated with toxic by-products. Thus, prohibition exposes illicit drug users to major health problems which taxpayers must pay to alleviate. Illicit hard drugs like cocaine and heroin, produced and adulterated in risky conditions, cannot easily be tested for quality and toxicity. There are further detrimental health effects such as poisoning, death by overdose, bone fractures, car accidents, HIV, bronchitis, hepatitis, anti-social aggression, paranoia and psychosis. In many cases there is an apparent correlation between the use of prohibited drugs, health risks and legal issues related to such prohibition, economic and social cost. Simply put, it is a "domino theory" of co-related cause and effect.

6

PROHIBITION:
A PERSONAL AFFAIR

"I don't do drugs. I am drugs."

Salvador Dali

The subject of prohibition is a very personal affair for me. It is not necessarily a love story, but at least, with 20/20 hindsight it is an exciting one. My introduction to prohibition came about when my travels took me throughout most of South America. As a younger man, I had previously traveled throughout Nicaragua, Guatemala and parts of Panama. This was an eyeopening experience for a young man who was looking to "discover himself and to find out where he came from." I can now say that no word description, however vivid, and no photograph, however true, can give a clear concept of the overwhelming obstacles that had to be overcome to make the Andean Sierras accessible and habitable. I spent the next several years frequently travelling the high altitude of the Andean Sierras, learning about the indigenous culture. The harsh nature of the Sierras did not make my staying any easier. The high altitude of 4,860 meters above sea level–where I spent most of my time–made my breathing extremely difficult. The heavy rainfall, mudslides, dense vegetation and the prolonged social destruction caused by political unrest, would appear fit only for producing and sustaining a crime-infested and poverty-stricken people. Time after time, I kept returning to these areas, not having a rational reason for doing so. Something unexplainable was leading me back to South America. Was it because I was fascinated by the endurance of the indigenous people in overcoming their obstacles. Was it because of my fascination with the Inca culture or was it a death-wish which lead me to regions that no outsider would dare enter? Whatever the reasons were, if any of the above, I am here to tell a story that is personal and true, as my memory permits. One thing must be made clear. The story is not about me per se, rather it is about prohibition with a personal touch. You see, I was a bootlegger, a smuggler, a contrabandist, a forger of documents and a full member of the corruption scene. I also want to make it clear that I never became a drug dealer, nor have I ever used drugs or alcohol. This is not because I am a religious person. Far from it. Nor am I a moralist who passes judgement on others' chosen behaviour. My reasons for abstaining from drugs and booze has to do with my early memories of addiction with members of own my family. That`s all!

Prohibition is more than a legal term restricting a product or products deemed harmful. Prohibition is a politically inspired ideological system of prohibiting certain public behavior, a given dress codes, loose morals and ethical attitude. In present day Iran, Saudi Arabia and Afghanistan, prohibition is imposed on women's dress, public displays of affection, nudity, the use of alcohol or drugs, the consumption of certain foods, days of resting etc. Jewish kosher cooking prohibits mixing utensils in the preparation of foods or the mixing of wool with cotton in weaved garments. The historical roots of prohibition, therefore, are ingrained in religion, religious-inspired morality, or functions as a political "strong-arm" of governments. For more than 200 years, temperance has been an ideology of religious moral purification of perceived social ills. South America is a mixed-bag of every known or unknown religious cult. You may enter a village on Saturday and see all the stores closed and Sunday the same stores open for business. The Seventh Day Adventist religious cult has simply prohibited the Saturday shopping where they are a dominating force.

Prohibition in Peru, was a political decision put into effect between 1985 to 1993 by the leftist government of President Alan Garcia. Its after-effects lasted until 1995. Prohibition was placed on most imported processed foods and liquors, electronics and machinery parts. If you had them, you could consume them, but they could not longer be imported into the country. The reasons were multiple, both rational and irrational. But those reasons were not valid to the public, because prohibition was imposed upon them not by any natural causes, but by the ideological political decisions of the day. For people, it was a matter of feeding themselves and their families, not about winning the war of ideas between the US hegemony and Peruvian leftists. The political pressure on Peru increased further when the International Monetary Fund (IMF) insisted on monetary policies not welcomed by the Peruvian government. The background of Peruvian prohibition therefore was socio-political, not inspired by religious goals. By the time I arrived in Peru, in mid 1989, prohibition's restraints were already felt by the Peruvian society.

Prohibition is a monolithic block with fixed characteristics regardless in which country it is fully or partially imposed. When specific products are deemed necessary or popular by the public's demand, there will be those who are willing to supply them. The law of public demand is a lot stronger than a written law. The public's alcohol demand in the 1920's slowly chipped away the monolithic block of prohibition until it was repealed. The US Alcoholic Prohibition of 1920's was encased in religiosity and moralistic ideology. Moral arguments, however, work best in churches and synagogues, not in the market place. The Peruvian prohibition of 1985 was enclosed in an ideology which, in essence, was no different in its end-result. In both cases, the market's supply and demand was unregulated, and the public's anxiety artificially increased demand. Artificially lowering the availability of goods (supply) is done by hiding goods from the public until demand increases, as does the prices. Hoarding of goods also increases demand because the supply of goods cannot be met. Today's drug prohibition does not regulate supply and demand. This is because the supply of drugs is controlled by the drug traffickers, not by the consumers of drugs. The marketing principles of supply and demand is severed by the intrusion of law enforcement. Both supplier and consumers adopt secretive methods of conducting their mutually agreed exchange. Prohibition thus does not eliminate illegal transactions of suppliers and consumers.It simply reduces the supply sequence of drugs and increases the demand of drugs many times over. These market contradictions became notable to me every time I shopped. The supplier controlled the market at will, because the demand was far greater than the supply. A supplier would not sell you products if the police were present, nor would he/she sell you products if you were not willing to pay more than a normal price. During the Alcohol Prohibition of 1920's, smuggled Canadian whiskey was $6 per case at arrival in US and sold for more than $60 per case. Whether prohibition is restricted to a specific product or is wider, its fundamental characteristics are identical.

Prohibition then creates the opportunity for many who are willing to capitalize on the lack of orderly supply and distribution of goods. Chaos is the ultimate result of an unregulated market. Law enforcement officers who want to control the latter were paid off to look the other way. Those who wanted to capitalize and profit by the situation became illegal suppliers of prohibited goods. I was one of them, amongst many others. Criminal elements were already in place producing a suspicious quality of goods which were dressed-up to appear as imported goods. By the time I got involved, all the unscrupulous players were in place. I knew an unscrupulous person who mixed red-shell (crushed into a powder) with pure cinnamon in order to increase its volume. Another was producing marshmallows which were mixed with animal glue to provide elasticity. Thousands of these marshmallow bags were sold to children around the Peruvian capital. During the US Alcohol Prohibition of the 1920's, industrial alcohol was mixed with imported liquor from Canada or from the Caribbean Islands. It was sold to underground bars or for home consumption. Today, pure drugs are diluted with water-soluble chemicals to increase their volume and profitability. I became a contrabandist (smuggler), mostly of industrial primary products, that yielded more profits with as little work as possible. There was no need to dilute them because I had no industrial means to do so. Had I the industrial means to dilute them, I probably would have done it.

Criminality breeds criminality wherever offenders and law enforcement are occupying opposed battlegrounds. In large-scale drug trafficking, substantive amounts of money and drugs are seized. Human nature is what it is in regards to an opportunity to have a little more money than what you normally have. Seized drugs are resold to street-level dealers for a share of the profits. Seized money is "misplaced" which is blamed on accounting mistakes. Bribery is a silent sin which is part of the normal slip-up of honest cops. I knew a lawyer (cocaine addict) who bribed a judge to give out lighter sentences for her clients. During the US Alcohol Prohibition, persecutors, judges, policemen, prison guards and Treasury agents were bribed at will. During the Peruvian prohibition there were 16 governmental officials I had to appease in order to conduct my business. They were not evil persons. They were all family men who took care of their wives and children and provided them with extra income for their convenience. Being creatures of habit, humans are able to adapt to different situations for comfort and survival. Bribes of officials was not a new phenomenon in Peru. It just became more extensive and habitual under prohibition's encouragement for quick profit. I was one–amongst others–who were in a position to contribute to their delinquency. Bribes of customs and police officials were re-named "helping-hand" gifts in an attempt to alleviate any sense of criminality or moral guilt. Merchants who were not able or not willing to bribe an official could not conduct their normal business affairs. One must also remember that any sort of prohibited business conducted under legal prohibition has multiple side effects in the economy. During the Alcohol Prohibition of 1920, hundreds of thousands of men were employed running thousands of bars and nightclubs, as truck drivers, as distillers of industrial alcohol etc. These businesses had their own economic side effects, whether their marketing activities were legal or illegal. Present day drug trafficking–especial the multi-billion dollar trade of marijuana–has its own direct or indirect national economic side effects. In these cases, the only losers are the taxpayers who do not benefit from collecting taxes.

My personal experience with prohibition includes more than just making money through victimless but illegal means. Being a habitual thinker, I had a first-hand opportunity to analyse prohibition and its compulsive corruption and criminality. I concluded that beyond the strict definition of legalities or illegalities of prohibition, beyond the competing elements within it, beyond the law enforcements' successes or failures, beyond the unwilling "partners" of the crime/law dichotomy, the real human tragedy were the people suffering from its implementation. In 2009, there were over 1,789.000 persons in the US who were imprisoned for marijuana offences. Thirty billion dollars was wastefully spent on the war on drugs. Think for a moment if the US declared a war on poverty. What could be done with 30 billion dollars a year, if invested in inner-cities, school structures and re-building abandoned houses for community use? There are millions of Americans who are using recreational drugs, and at the same time paying for the law enforcement against the use of those.

Prohibition is a 100% wasteful physical effort. It is politically supported by a minority of misguided puritanical religious moralists or by equally misguided politicians. It is both socially wasteful for those who are fighting to enforce prohibition and for those who take risks to profit from it. Prohibition is a set of circumstantial opportunities unwillingly created for the exclusive benefit of the law enforcement militarized industry, and the criminal parasites who define the law. Professional advancement, economic benefits, family planning and vocations are essentially identical for activists on opposites sides of the law. Ideological justification for or against the unwilling "partners" of prohibition, not including the material elimination of their existence, is a never-ending futile academic exercise. Drug trafficking and related criminal activities are practiced for non-ideological reasons. Rather, the players in the criminal field of prohibition are guided by monetary gains. Their opponents are guided by their professional vested self-interests. I am stating my views, without cynicism, hostility or malice. I give my greatest personal warmth to the brave law enforcement officers who are against drug prohibition. These brave men and women have put the interest of the citizens over their own. They have done so without regard to the self-served organizational goals of the law enforcement system.

Prohibition, like natural disasters, creates desperate circumstances. Human beings cannot control the consequences caused by such circumstances. Different people may react without qualifying their actions as being "good" or "bad". Personal traits suddenly appear to activate one's internal safety valve of " fight or flight"(to use a psychological jargon). To flee is to co-operate and do the best for one's self or family. Millions of recreational drug users and drug addicts have fled into the bosoms of their habits. Activists for the legalization of drugs are fighting for the decriminalization of all those who are using drugs. Persecuting, imprisoning and criminally stigmatising drug addicts simply adds to their existing misery caused by their medical problem. During Peruvian prohibition thousands of "little people" fought prohibition measures by entering the small-scale trading of consumer goods. Hundreds of run-down busses were chartered to travel to the southern part of Peru to purchase goods that were smuggled in from Chile. The 2,400 km round trip was not a pleasant experience. With no bus bathroom facilities, no air conditioning and not enough space in them–due to the volume of merchandise–those busses were mobile death coffins. Human perspiration and bodily smells could not be avoided because bus windows were permanently sealed. Frequent mechanical breakdowns, drivers falling asleep causing tragic accidents, were not uncommon. Merchandise would be hidden along the 1,200 km to be picked up by others who delivered them to highland communities. Before busses entered the capital of Lima, merchants would get off to hide their goods in the desert. Thus, they were avoiding the cost of bribing the officials at the final highway control point. This Pan-American Highway was an infamous road to travel. Highway robbers and mountain bandits, narco-terrorists, renegade police and army groups were all extorting money or robbing bus passengers. I witnessed a single policeman, with his gun drown, stopping a bus and collecting token "fees" from everyone. I also contributed to his "request". At night, busses and private vehicles formed convoys for their own protection against unforeseen dangers. The above is the typical social environment of prohibition. During the US Alcohol Prohibition of 1920, highway robbers were a common phenomenon. Every truck carrying bootlegged booze or moonshine was subject to robbery from competing groups or bandits. Policemen and other patrolmen would be bribed to allow trucks to continue on their way. Thousands of unemployed men were "mule" carriers of moonshine and bootlegged alcohol. They made a meager living, just like the Peruvian men and women I have witnessed. Today, the drug trade is not a peaceful occupation. Deceit, rip-offs, robberies, raids of marijuana growing plots, extorting "mules" of the drugs they carry and out-right murder, are all part of the drug prohibition environment. It is a desperate and hostile environment where desperate men, desperate for drugs, money or both, do desperate things.

My time as a medium-scale smuggler and bootlegger permitted me to meet a variety of different kinds of characters. Doing what I was doing for little more than five years, I saw the goodness, the weakness and the nastiness of men like myself. I saw the victims and the predators of prohibition. No one could escape from such a culture without being marked for life. I became less sensitive to others, but still maintained a sense of humanity. My opinion of man is a bit ironic (if that's the right word). I formed the opinion that under extreme circumstances, hidden personal traits appear to project the kind of human a person is or can be. As for the good, the weak and the nasty, I attributed those qualities to my metaphorical man. I have seen nasty men because they were weak and needed to hide their weakness by being nasty. For my own mental convenience, I separated men into two kinds: the "good" man who was far too weak to become a nasty man, and the true good man who was good by choice, while he could turn nasty when needed. I considered myself a good man by choice. I was revisiting my old "play-grounds" of Peru when the earthquake hit in August 2007. This tragic event brought the best out of me, for I was able to help old friends re-build their adobe homes. This was my redemption! Yes, it was! The rest is history.

7

PHOTO TOUR
OF FACTS & PROPAGANDA
1820 - 1937

"See, in my line of work you got to keep repeating things over and over again for the truth to sink in...to kind of catapult the propaganda."

George W. Bush - May 24, 2005

The term *propaganda* implies a sinister impression involving a subversive falsehood. An accurate definition of propaganda is given in the *Oxford English Dictionary* as "any association, systematic scheme, or concentrated movement for the propagation of a particular doctrine or practice." Thus, propaganda is generally perceived as a negative instrument for striking false notions of moralistic consequences, depending on its authors and their aims. Fundamentalist religious and moralist groups systematically employ an entire range of propaganda media–writing, filming, public speaking–to rouse the public to fanatical assent. The propaganda in support of the prohibition of alcohol and drugs in the early 20th century was a drive to demonize alcohol and recreational drugs, and cast as a war the transcendent clash between the Protestant and Puritan's version of morality and the liberal immorality that must be destroyed.

Many of the drugs now restricted by legislation were legal up until the early 1900's and most required no prescription, for they were indeed available over the counter, sold by all druggists. Cocaine, marijuana and opiates were legal and not considered harmful in moderate doses. Opium use was construed as an eccentric pastime of a few middle and upper-class "softies", whereas the drinking of the working and ghetto men was considered an urgent public problem of addiction. A broad distinction in the levels of drunkenness was made between the public and private consumption of alcohol. What annoyed the religious puritans was that drunkenness took place in public and thus geared their attention to certain classes of people who drank in public or went about drunk. Of course, drunkenness was not a crime, but public drunkenness and rowdiness was seen as an "uncivilized" nuisance of the poor who seemed to be having too much fun. As for the middle class, they tended to drink privately in order to maintain their social status of civility. The temperance campaigns against drinking alcohol had little to do with an epidemic of drunkenness, and more to do with middle-class puritanical ideas. Taking a drink with one's family, participation in religious activities, the ideology of self-respect, personal and moral prudence was opposite to the working-class public entertainment of bar-hopping.

BEFORE PROHIBITION

The following images are from the pre-prohibition era when many psychotropic drugs were legally available over the counter or just for the asking. Unfortunately some pictures are not in high resolution and others are not very clear.

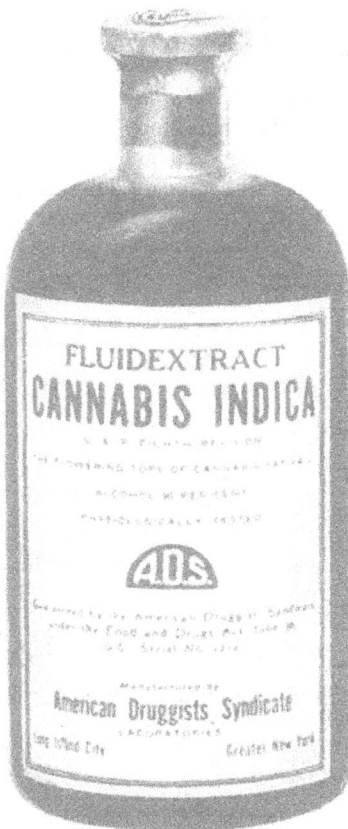

PRODUCTS CONTAINING COCAINE

Many manufacturers of drugs and several beverage companies produced products containing potent drug compounds like opium or cocaine. This was as common a practice in the 19th and 20th century as it is today. Many 19th century manufacturers proudly proclaimed that their products contained opiates.

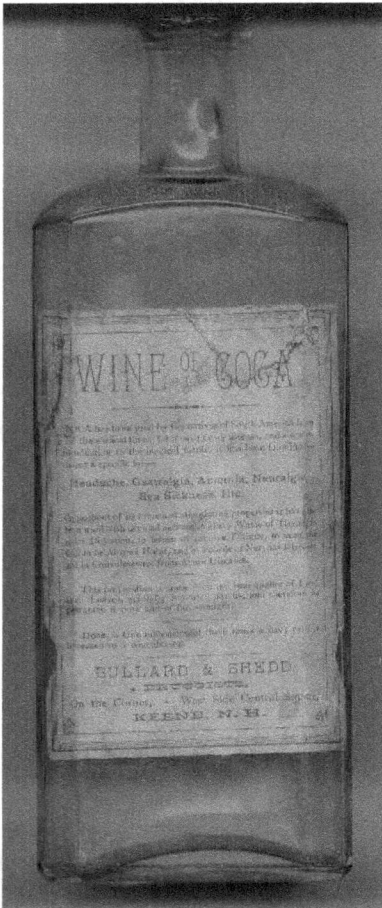

This Coca wine was promoted by the Maltine Manufacturing Co. of New York. Its directional use indicates "a wine glass full with, or immediately after, meals. Children in proportion."

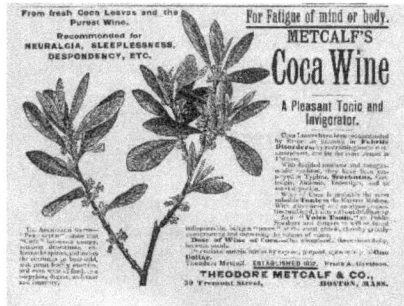

Metcalf's Coca Wine was one of many Coca wines available on the market. It was promoted for it health effects, and for its recreational value as well.

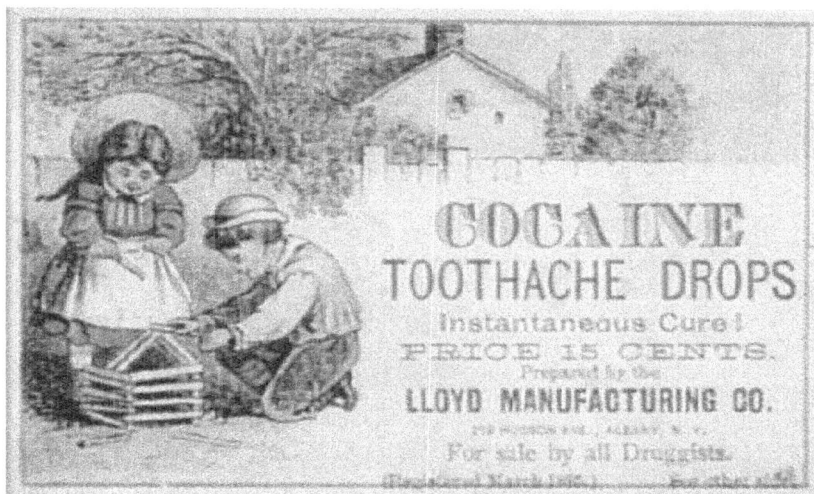

Cocaine was used as an effective local anaesthetic. The earliest uses of cocaine included the mood-elevating and euphoric feeling that can occur with cocaine.

c. 1906 Coca-Cola Syrup listing ingredients. When coca leaves became illegal, the Coca-Cola Co. Syrup was still sold for its medical effects. Today, the Coca-Cola Co. uses de-cocainized coca leaves as one of the ingredients used for its popular beverage.

Revised Retail Prices of
COCA WINE.
ARMBRECHT'S
FOR FATIGUE OF MIND AND BODY.
NEURALGIA,
SLEEPLESSNESS,
DESPONDENCY,

TWELVE BOTTLES, 44s.   TWENTY-FOUR BOTTLES, 84s.

Professional Price: 40s. per dozen; 21s. half-dozen.

ARMBRECHT, NELSON & CO.,
2, Duke St., Grosvenor Square, London. W.

In addition to endorsements from celebrities, physicians and scientists, Pope Leo XIII also endorsed the popular product for its beneficial effects.

Contemporary 0.05mg Cocaine-Containing Beverages: using de-cocainized coca leaves as main ingredients of their energy drinks.

Prescription form for medicinal liquor:

French Tonic Wine:

Paperweight advertisement for
C.F. Boehringer & Soehne
(Mannheim , Germany):

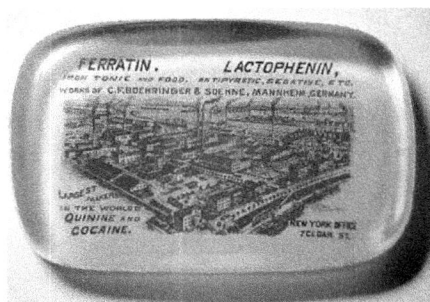

19th century Coca wine advertisement:

Legal production of Marijuana – 1945:

RELIGIOUS PROPAGATED TEMPERANCE MOVEMENT 1820-1920

I never knew I had a wonderful wife until the town went dry. 1919

THE DEFENDER OF THE 18TH AMENDMENT

DRUG PROHIBITION PROPAGANDA

Prohibition is a social condition propagated by racism, fear, ignorance, incompetence, corrupt politicians, corporate greed and personal career advancement. Prohibitionists use propaganda against the public's personal habits that are not in line with their own fundamentalist dogma. They do not base their arguments on rational processes involving scientific, medical evidence and public hearings by qualified individuals. They are motivated by their political agenda and use deceptive propaganda to achieve their goals. In fact, it would not be an exaggeration to say that state and federal legislators are far more influenced by the hypocritical double standard of the religious fundamentalists than by the people they represent.

By the early 1900's, the western states bordering with Mexico were under significant tension regarding the influx of Mexican-American descent. This tension was due to the perceived differences between the two cultures. One was the perception that Mexicans smoked marijuana and imported the hemp plant into the US. Any bad feeling against Mexican-Americans was translated also against the "loco weed" i.e., marijuana. This problem was affiliated with Latin Americans, as well as with Black jazz musicians, since marijuana was an indispensable part of the popular music scene, and the linguistic expression of the jazz hit songs of the time. Racism against Blacks and Mexicans was part of the anti-marijuana propaganda and songs by Luis Armstrong such as "Muggles" or Cab Calloway's "That Funny Reefer Man" were translated into the racists' fears of the evil weed. Comments like "Marijuana influences Negroes to look at white people in the eye, step on white man's shadows and look at a white woman twice" were at the core of the racial fear. Other propaganda quotes are attributed to the first director of the Bureau of Narcotics, H. Anslinger, a shadowy figure. The racism inherent in his quotes are self evident:

"There are 100,000 total marijuana smokers in the US, and most are Negroes, Hispanics, Filipinos, and entertainers. Their Satanic music, jazz, and swing, result from marijuana use. This marijuana causes white women to seek sexual relations with Negroes, entertainers, and any others"..."

"...the primary reason to outlaw marijuana is its effect on the degenerate races."

"Marijuana is an addictive drug which produces in its users insanity, criminality, and death."

"Reefer makes darkies [blacks] think they're as good as white men."

"You smoke a joint and you're likely to kill your mother."

MEDIA PROPAGANDA

William Randolph Hearst, owner of a conglomerate chain of newspapers in the US, used his power and influence to sway public opinion to his liking. Hearst had good reasons to fear the hemp-plant. Hemp is a quickly renewable source of fibre that can be used to produce paper, including newsprint. Hearst had invested heavily in the wood pulp industry, a primary source for his newspaper chain, and he didn't want the hemp-fibre undermining his investment. He also hated Mexicans because he had lost hundreds of thousands of primary woodland to the revolutionary Pancho Villa. Above all, he knew how to sell daily newspapers by creating sensational news, thus making himself a millionare many times over. Propaganda against the hemp (marijuana) served him well economically, industrially and racially. He told lurid lies in his *San Francisco Examiner* editorials:

"Users of marijuana become stimulated as they inhale the drug and are likely to do anything. Most crimes of violence in this

section, especially in country districts are laid to users of the drug."

"Was it marijuana, the new Mexican drug, that nerved the murderous arm of Clara Phillips when she hammered out her victim's life in Los Angeles?...three-fourths of the crimes of violence in the country today are committed by dope slaves—that is a matter of cold record."

In other editorials:

"Marijuana makes friends of boys [turning them gay] in thirty days–Hashish goads users to bloodlust."

"By the tons [marijuana] it is coming into this country–the deadly, dreadful poison that racks and tears not only the body, but the very heart and soul of every human being who once becomes a slave to it in any of its cruel and devastating forms...Marijuana is a short cut to the insane asylum. Smoke marijuana...for a month and what was once your brain will be nothing but a storehouse of horrid specters. Hashish makes a murderer who kills for the love of killing out of the mildest mannered men who ever laughed at the idea that any habit could ever get him..."

William Randolph Hearst

Anslinger

A prominent opponent of such distorting claims was Dr. William C. Woodward, of the Legislative Council of the American Medical Association, stating that those claims were not endorsed by the AMA., as was suggested by Anslinger and Hearst.

COCA LEAF PRODUCTS

Bolivia's capital, Le Paz, is the home of the world's only historical museum dedicated to the coca plant. In Peru and Bolivia coca products (not cocaine) are legal and used as tea or ice-tea. Chewing coca leaves or drinking coca tea brings more oxygen to the brain and helps relieve the effects of altitude sickness.

Below are varieties of coca tea that I have personally used for more than 10 years. These products are produced by La Empresa National de la Coca, of Peru.

Manzanilla con Coca
(Apple with Coca)

Hierba Luisa con
Coca
(Coca with
Lemongrass)

Menta con Coca
(Mint with Coca)

Mate de Coca
(Coca-Tea)

8

IN THE SHADOW OF DRUG PROHIBITION

"Let us revise our views and work from the premise that all laws should be for the welfare of society as a whole and not directed at the punishment of sins."

John Biggs Jr.

There are many reasons why someone writes a book. It may be an academic exercise, a biography or a fictional story from someone's imagination. All are valid reasons. There is, of course, one other reason which makes the task of writing worthwhile: to tell the truth about human affairs caused by prohibition. In my case, I was a player in the shadow of prohibition and an active participant in it, for profit. Now, if you ever pass by me on the street, you would never look at me twice. I fit into the typical cliché of the polite Canadian who does not attract attention. I am an artist and a writer. Yet, when I was confronted with the realism of personal survival, I discovered that I had hidden "talents" and creativity for illegal activities. I had to be creative in order to survive under Prohibition. Nowadays, I am very happy to be back to my old typical cliché of the polite Canadian. This is a true story of a smuggler, bootlegger, forger and a black market operator, under the shadow of prohibition.

Prohibition has four main affects:

❖ it raises prices, disrupts market functioning and prevents the open promotion of products.

❖ it sacrifices the authorities' ability to tax transactions and regulate operations of the market, product characteristics (quality) and promotional activities of suppliers.

❖ it fails to control the harmful use of contaminated material integrated into food products consumed by children and adults.

❖ it creates conditions of corruption at every level of civil society including the custom service, police, national guard, taxation officials and in other government bodies.

My first encounter with the effects of prohibition was the day after I arrived in Lima, the capital of Peru, South America. I entered an outwardly impressive supermarket in a classy neighbourhood to purchase needed items. I say classy neighbourhood because the people living in this area were mostly non-indigenous or of European descent who tended to be the leaders in business and political life. While I was walking around looking for items, I noticed that most of the shelving rows were empty of groceries. When I asked an employee to direct me to my desired items, I was told that I can have "whatever is on the shelves" . What was on the shelves were 30 lb bags of rice, 20 lb bags of beans and cans of Peruvian fish. In a short time, I was approached by an employee who offered to sell me a jar of imported peanut butter for $20 US. He was a "freelance" entrepreneur within the supermarket that was employing him in the first place. The price for the medium-size peanut butter jar was exorbitant. When I opened the jar at home, I noticed that the "peanut butter" was something other than peanut butter. Much later, I found out that there were people whose job it was to collect jars, food containers, medicine bottles like aspirin, discarded medicine bottles from hospitals, lotion containers etc. They would in turn sell those to various "manufacturers" of falsified medicines or other items, and sell them as genuine products in their original packages. My "peanut butter", therefore, was one of those products that contained little peanut butter but was mixed (for volume) with other kinds of material. Imitations of medicine were made with colour/starch and were re-packaged in their original containers. I could only imagine cancer patients, whose lives dependened upon the "medicines" they purchased who were now dying from this ineffective "medicine".

The prohibition on the importation of most products including medicine, food, electronics etc, was twofold. First, no foreign currency (held in the Peruvian Banks) was allowed to be used to pay for any kind of imported goods.

Secondly, only foreign currency that was located outside the Peruvian Banking system could be used for purchasing and importing goods. It should be noted that all foreign currency accounts were confiscated by the government of the day, and were replaced by Peruvian "soles" that held no monetary value in other countries.

This is a typical condition of prohibition. It creates a black market for criminals with money to smuggle goods that people need or want. In addition, prohibition creates a second criminal element of contraband producers of goods that are of inferior quality and dangerous to consumers. When I refer to "goods" this term may apply to medicine, rot-gut liquor, recreational drugs, food or whatever is deemed forbidden under prohibition. For example, during the US 1920's Prohibition, there were bootleggers who produced moonshine, adulterated rum and whisky, that poisoned hundreds of drinkers who could not afford the prices of legally produced (but smuggled) Canadian or Caribbean liquor. In my five years as a smuggler and bootlegger in Peru, I "imported" hundreds of cases of legally produced liquor from the Free Zone of Iquique, Chile. I had to smuggle them out of Chile and smuggle them again out of the Peruvian Custom Service, once the cases were in its custody. The destination of my goods was 1,500 km away a treacherous trip full of highway robbers, police blockades, custom service inspectors of truck and cars, etc. By bribes, gifts and promises to all the powers that be, the shipments arrived in Lima to be sold within 24 hours at a 1000% profit margin.

My point is that during the Alcohol Prohibition of the 1920's, the price of smuggled liquor was also exorbitant, for the cost of corruption, en route to the black market, was very expensive, and so was the smuggler's greed. This is also true with today's smuggling of illegal drugs. Today, after more than 95 years of imposed Drug Prohibition, recreational narcotics are smuggled en route to US and European illegal markets. Knowing what I know, the quality of these drugs is questionable, if not outright dangerous to the health of the drug users. It is common knowledge that the price of smuggled drugs is exorbitant. The cost of cultivating a single plant of marijuana in Mexico or Jamaica is no more than $2 per plant. Yet, the end product may be sold in the illegal market for an exorbitant price. Greed for exorbitant profits is the most singular reason that one will enter the "business" of drug production and smuggling. Period.

So, who are the losers during Prohibition? From the viewpoint of the public health, it is the youth and the drug addicted who are ignorant or who have no choice but to consume adulterated and contaminated narcotics. Whether those products are smuggled or produced nationally, there is no quality control, no measurement and no rules of transportation and storage. Illicit drugs, by their nature and means of production, are inherently mixed with harmful substances. They are mixed with cutting agents to increase their volume, or generically diluted to increase their potency. In the case of the liquor that I was "importing", once the whisky or rum was consumed, the discarded bottles were purchased by those whose 'business' was to refill them with tea-coloured adulterated alcohol to be resold in poor neighbourhoods. Periodically, the Peruvian local news would report mass scale liquor poisoning, enough to fil the emergency rooms of local hospitals and clinics. In our "civilized" society, we also have those who suffer from gradual or sudden drug poisoning and need to be hospitalized for overdosing and for other health complications. The lack of unit quality and measurement control causes a public health problem. In 2008, close to a million persons received medical treatment for the use of illicit drugs. Some 4 million youth aged 12 or older received medical treatment for both alcohol and drugs. I believe that the contaminated cutting agents used by the drug dealers in our country are far more addictive than the purity of the un-adulterated drugs. The cutting agents used in the illicit drug process are no less contaminated than the industrial-alcohol cutting agent used by bootleggers in Peru. Recognizing the historical chronology of drug use, I say that recreational drugs are here to stay. We can either deal with their addictive medical effects in a rational way or follow a policy of delusional moralistic righteousness: the War on Drugs.

Prohibition is not just selective to a body's dietary consumption–like food or drugs–it applies also to industry and commerce. My friend Pablo (not his real name) was a successful importer of household items until his bank account of American dollars was converted to Peruvian "soles". He no longer had a foreign-exchange currency to pay for his importations. This simply put an end to his business. Some time later, he decided to change his current position. One of his most popular imported products was different styles of irons for ironing clothes. So Pablo traveled to Miami, Florida, and purchased samples of irons and set out to copy them in Peru. More follows.

The liquor smuggling trade, in the meantime, was getting more intensive between various groups about prices and customers. It was time for me to get out of the booze business. Like the old saying, "When the little guy goes in, the smart guy gets out." I decided to look for other smuggling opportunities. Following some rumours–and confirming that they were true–I decided to "import" industrial nickel used for the electrolysis of utensils, bicycle wheels, or any metal surface that needed a shiny coating, including irons. There were a number of cottage-industry electrolysis shops that served the needs of the 8 million inhabitants of Lima. One of those who needed the services of electrolysis was none other than Pablo. You see, Pablo was successful in producing copies of his irons, and he needed to have the bottoms of his irons nickel-coated. He was producing them by the thousands, but he had trouble securing the services of electrolysis due to a shortage of the primary material: nickel. That is, until he meet me. I already had the logistical structure of the smuggling operation; he had the need for the primary material. The basic market conditions of supply and demand were there–with one exception. Due to prohibition, the supply of the material was prohibited, and thus it was illegal. I was a smuggler and thus a criminal. I was a forger of commercial invoices and thus I was a criminal. I was a briber of corrupt government officials (16 in total) and thus a criminal. I paid not a single dime in taxes and thus I was a tax-evader which was a felony under the law.

Prohibition and corruption go hand to hand. Prohibition leads to the unregulated quality of products. Pablo's irons–though they looked good-had unsafe electrical components. After a number of uses, the iron's electrical wiring would burn out and they needed constant repairs. I am not the only one who can see the qualitative relationship between adulterated liquor, adulterated drugs and the poor qualitative workmanship of Pablo's irons. I am not the only one who claims that criminals are made not born. In fact, prohibition breeds crime which, in turn, breeds more crime. There was a price on my head offered by a major competitor of smuggled nickel/chemicals, who simply wanted the *"Maldito Gringo-Canadiense"* dead.

During the years of prohibition, there were hundreds of thousands of micro-smugglers involved in the supply and demand of contraband goods. Small scale farmers, day workers, wife/husband teams, the young, the old and the very old became micro-smugglers. Small street-stands were set-up every morning to sell contraband goods. Some street vendors sold adulterated foods called "slow-death", pickpockets thrived, policemen were bribed to let the street vendors stay-put, micro-drug dealers sold and smoked "pasta de coca" in the open, private bodyguards were in high demand, and everyone's daily life was brutish, nasty and short. A widespread 'culture of crime' became more vivid with the appearance of professional forgers who 'issued' government "Importation Permits" to street vendors, thus preventing custom inspectors from confiscating their meagre goods. Street vendors, the manufacturers of adulterated medicine, liquor and food were making a "killing" in profits. The human environment called society was a social jungle! This was also a War on Contraband, where the police department had its paramilitary units blockading urban areas in search of contraband. There were no-knock entries into private homes and businesses. In the 1920's, the US Prohibition had a narrow scope (drugs, alcohol). Still, the law enforcement's paramilitary style that applied search and destroy methods were similar to the ones I witnessed in Peru. Today, the US and Canadian Drug Squads operate in a similar paramilitary style when searching homes of suspected drug dealers.

This is a paramilitary war against offenders who were themselves created by the laws of prohibition, a war against civil liberties, and a war that makes all citizens very uncomfortable. Things were getting a bit too dangerous for my wife Cecilia and my newborn daughter Melissa. Not so much from my trade activities–I was the only one who was exposed to nastiness–but from the general state of Peruvian affairs. Lawlesness was a permanent state of affairs caused by prohibition and by related criminal activities. The political violence among the government and the Maoist rebel forces of the Sendero Luminoso (Shining Path) and the Revolutionary Movement Tupak Amaru (MRTA) was getting too close for comfort. Far too many bombs were exploded within a very short distance from my family. The front of a commercial bank was bombed as we passed less than 100 ft away from it. Another time, waiting in a traffic jam, I noticed that two men were placing a long pipe (through a chain link fence) into a car lot. The pipes exploded, sending American made cars 20ft up in the air. I happened to have my driver's window open, and I felt the force of the exploded hot air on my face. But what drove me out of Lima to the northern city of Arica, Chile was this. It was one of those beautiful days and I was playing with my 18 month old daughter Melissa. We were both in front of our 8th floor apartment window looking at the city scenery when the Bolivian Embassy was bombed less than half a block away. Smoke, debris, the smell of burning and our building's tremors scared the hell out of me. A few days later, I was sitting in an outdoor café when the ground shook violently from an explosion. A car bomb exploded in Tarrata street killing 45 people, wounding several hundred and destroying most of the buildings on both sides of the street. The following week, we moved to the city of Arica, Chile.

The city of Arica is the commercial centre of the Andean Triangle of Chile, Bolivia and Peru. It is a 24/7 cross-border human passage for merchant trade, tourism and drug trafficking activity. The traditional cultivation of coca plants is visible everywhere. Coca leaves are bought and sold in bundles of 50 lbs freely and openly. Because of the Peruvian Prohibition, smuggling of goods from Chile to the Peruvian border city of Tacna was a daily activity. At night, the Peruvian border patrols would be at the desert look-out to prevent trafficking of goods and drugs. Smuggling and liquor bootlegging was regarded as a job, something one does for a living to support one's family. I now was living 1,500 km south of Lima and in a relatively safer place. I no longer needed to commute between Tacna and Lima to transport my contraband goods. It did not take me long to find corrupt airline cargo personnel, in Tacna, to fly my goods to Lima (with no Bill of Landing). Because of the drastic prohibition restraints, it was common to find people here from Lima looking for someone to do [one time] smuggling on their behalf.

A respectable geriatric doctor from Lima approached me seeking my "help" to smuggle a particular product. The good doctor operating a number of old age homes whose residents needed adult diapers. This product was under prohibition by the laws of the land. Yet, this product was part of the health care provided to old people with unique needs. The elderly faced health problems relating to incontinence. In order to solve such a medical necessity, the good doctor was forced to break the law and thus become an offender! Please think of this for a moment. How many of our teens are forced to become offenders and face criminal charges because, for medical reasons, they may need illegal drugs? The products may be different, but, in both cases, it is one of necessity. In those days, I was not noted for being a sentimental man. But after hearing the doctor's pleas, I decided to truly help him acquire his product. The main problem was that the adult diapers were very bulky. Each box contained four cases of diapers. The boxes were not heavy, just bulky. After much planning, the good doctor travelled 2000 km south to Santiago de Chile, and legally purchased a full tractor-trailer of adult diapers right from the manufacturer. We rented a warehouse in Arica and stored them.

It was now up to me to find a way to smuggle the diapers out of Chile and re-smuggle them into Peru, followed by transporting them over 1,500 km north to Lima. The border distance between Arica and the Tacna desert was approximately 15 km. It was a common phenomenon to have smugglers and bootleggers from both countries walk this distance, carrying their goods on their backs. Sra Govinda (not her real name) was one of the women who would frequently walk this distance. Women from both sides of the border were the "mules" who performed smuggling services for others. That was their job, and that was how they made their living. They would simply carry their cargo and by-pass the border guard posts on the way to their destinations. I contracted Sra Govinda who sub-contracted 40 other women of her village, to carry two boxes each to just inside the Peruvian borders. In three days, the job was complete. The boxes were stored with a Peruvian-Chinese family--father, mother and a dozen kids,-- who worked diligently to hide the boxes in the terrace of their home, out of sight of the curious eyes of others and the police. It did not take me long to find a secure means of transportation–destination, the old people's longterm care homes of Lima, Peru. Screw the government's prohibition! This act of good will was my repentance! Even my wife, who did not like what I was doing before, was now cheering for me in a semi-content fashion.

A few months later, I was approached by a military intelligence officer while I was visiting the border city of Tacna. He said that he wanted to talk to me, and could I have lunch with him. During the lunch hour, he said that he was given an order by his superiors to have me transferred to Lima. I was to meet with someone there who had accused me of taking part in illegal activities. What was strange about this, was that I was not to be taken to a law enforcement body, but to meet someone who supposedly accused me of being part of illegal activities. Casually, I asked for the name of my accuser. He gave me the name of my competitor in Lima, the one who was looking to put an end to the nickel problem. Of course, there were no "superiors" that had ordered him to get me to Lima. I was to be delivered to my competitor for an unceremonial ending. This was typical of prohibition's "dog eat dog" crime climate to eliminate one's turf competitors. After I scared the hell out of the officer by dropping the names of various upper level military and police brass who were working with me, I gave him $100 and sent him away. Much later, I found out that the officer reported that he could not find me because I was no longer in Peru. This was the worst side of prohibition's culture of crime and corruption.

The War on Drugs took place in the jungles, valleys and highlands of Peru, Bolivia and Colombia. I am not overly familiar with the Colombian situation on the war on drugs. I am more familiar with the consequences of the war on drugs taking place within the Andean Triangle of Peru, Bolivia and northern Chile. As well, this was the epicentre of narco-terrorists operating in the southern interior of Peru. Having moved to the Chilean city of Arica, my daily life was split commuting between the two cities. Being so near to Bolivia, I often flew to its capital of La Paz to cultivate connections for smuggling gold from the jungle of Potosí. At one point, my stay in the Bolivian jungle of Potosi lasted about 10 days. Leaving La Paz towards Potosi in a "kamikaze" jeep with a lunatic driver, I noticed that every few kilometres of the jungle road, paramilitary groups, mercenaries and strange-looking characters were conducting roadblock inspections. I recognized some of these mercenaries from a clandestine eatery in Lima. It was operated by an ex-mercenary Englishman whose eatery was also a gathering place for mercenaries. They gathered in clandestine out of fear that Sendero Luminoso rebels might bomb them. In other words, the eatery had no distinct markings on its outside structure. The war on drugs was planned there over drinks, drugs and the need to earn money. Their mission was to travel to different parts of Peru and Bolivia and to scout, destroy and kill anyone who was operating a "kitchen" for the production of cocaine. For a standard fee of $200 US per day (tax free?), these mercenaries (paid by who knows whom) were conducting their war on drugs by destroying and killing. Though most of them were dope addicts themselves, they didn't seem to have any conflict with killing those who produced their dope in the Bolivian and Peruvian jungles. Any finished drug product was confiscated by them...ha! My trip into the jungle of Potosi was a success, even though I didn't acquire any contraband gold. My trip was a success simply because I got out of there alive, for I had no chance of getting out in one piece while carrying gold on me. During my short visit to the jungle, I noticed an unfamiliar smell in the air. It was neither sweet nor bitter. Nor was the smell in one area and not in another. It was strong in the day and night, inside the jungle or in the villages. I paid no further attention to the smell until I arrived back at Arica's airport. A friend who met me there commented that I smelled like cocaine, and that my clothes smelled of cocaine. You see, the jungle of Potosi was a main cocaine production area, which explained the smell in the entire environment, and the concentration of paramilitary and mercenary forces in that area.

Daily life under prohibition was getting worse in Peru. Corruption caused by the restrictions of prohibition was rampant; the micro-smugglers were suffering the most. Street gangs had control of their turf and any micro-smuggler (street vendor) had to pay them to sell his goods. Next came the municipal inspectors who charged the vendors a dollar or two per day to let them stay on. Vendors would receive a municipal receipt for half of the amount paid; the balance was pocketed by the municipal inspectors. Next came the police patrol, who were "the bottom of the barrel." The constant music from vendors of CDs, garbage litter caused by food vendors, lack of toilet facilities, pickpockets, dope vendors, prostitutes, child beggars, and "boosters" re-selling what they previously had stolen all created the perception of a lawless society. Due to the prohibition on the importation of foreign goods, national taxation and importation duties had declined. The government had no money to invest in social programs, pensioners were not receiving what was due to them, and government workers were forced to work with no pay for months at a time. Electrical power blackouts, for homes, businesses and traffic lights lasted for months at a time. In the city of 8 million, the vehicle traffic chaos cause by blackouts also caused a concentration of air pollution from cars with their engines idling. The city water supply and the purification process that needed electrical power to run was effected as well. The only sectors of society that thrived were the bootleggers and smugglers of contraband goods like myself. This sector of offenders could afford to buy anything they wanted that they were not smuggling. They could afford to buy smuggled generators to hook-up power for their homes and refrigerators, for air conditioners and electrical water purifiers. Imported foods were available in abundance because they had the money to pay for them. That was, until the presidential election of Alberto Fujimory.

As a presidential candidate, Fujimori had openly declared an end to the prohibition on the importation of any goods and services. I saw Fujimori as a pragmatic politician who, among other national issues, saw that prohibition was one of the gravest of issues needing to be solved. The Peruvian state needed free market principles, the organized collection of taxes on goods and services and prices to be regulated by supply and demand. The production and quality of goods including medicine and foods for public consumption, needed safety guidelines. Society's Law and Order needed be based on the rational implementation of citizens' justice and human rights protection especially for those who were most vulnerable.

As for me, I could see how Fujimori's election would affect my contraband business. Liberating trade and commerce for all is the "last nail in the coffin" of smuggling, mass corruption and related social ills. Was I sad to see such "promising" criminal activity ending with no fanfare? Clearly, I was not. This was because I had taken my 'revenge' by making back the thousands of dollars I had been cheated of by crooked Peruvian businessmen. As well, I had lost my stained glass and etching studio in Toronto, Canada. That was when I had first arrived in Peru, more than seven years previously. I had ended up sleeping on someone's couch, with Cecilia pregnant and with $3 US in my pocket. And, a lot of personal shame to boot! Before the end of prohibition, I sold out my contraband stock and closed "shop" with no moral implications for or against what I had been doing.

With the declaration of the end of prohibition, and liberation from the constraints of illegality, slowly things began to change in Peru. Bootleggers and large-scale smugglers began to disappear; most of them turned into legitimate businessmen. Micro-smugglers no longer made the kind of profits they were making under prohibition. They were still in business as street vendors, trying to sell off their old stock. Fewer and fewer of them continued to block off the streets by setting-up shop anywhere they pleased. Garbage became less and less visible, the smell of street urine became less noticeable.

Within a few short months, large scale supermarkets began to operate 24/7, providing consumers with clean and safe food, medical prescriptions and so on. Large-scale wholesalers forced local food producers to follow standard quality control in their production of dairy, vegetable, poultry and meat supplies. I know this, because the end of prohibition also transformed me into a legitimate businessman supplying some 35 supermarkets with health-inspected goods. Once again I saw consumers with shopping carts–husbands, wives and families with children–selecting their goods in the same supermarkets that I supplied. It was time for me and my family to return back home to Canada.

In 2007, I returned to Peru for an extensive visit. Things had progressed so much that I saw streets I had never noticed before. This was because these same streets were now clean, orderly and free of all the nasty street vendors that had once clogged the same streets. I was still in Peru in August of 2007 when the earthquake happened, killing several hundred people. I, once again, survived such a catastrophe for the third time. In 2008, I returned to Peru to help an old fried rebuild his home. Peru still has its problems, as does everywhere else in this world. But the social ills, the human tragedy and corruption that was present under prohibition no longer exists.

The lessons that I have learned by being a smuggler, an illegal profit-maker of basic human necessities, a bootlegger and a corruptor of those who held public trust is invaluable. I do not treat prohibition, at any level, as an academic exercise. I have closely seen and lived the negative effects that prohibition had on people. Exorbitant prices caused financial and emotional difficulties on people who had no other option but to pay what was demanded of them. Adulterated products were slowly poisoning poor people who had no other choice but to buy what the illegal producers were selling to them. Adulterated medicines, which had no medical effect on the sick and elderly, were the worst that I have ever seen. Nurses in the hospitals would substitute adulterated medicines for the real ones, and sell the real back to the other patients.

As for me, I was what the circumstances allowed me to become. But I have never sold any kind of drugs–real or adulterated, legal or illegal–nor have I ever sold adulterated foods to either poor or rich people. The goods that I smuggled and sold were for those who could afford to pay for luxury goods at my prices. The question is: are there people today who are like I was under the current state of drug prohibition? Are the personal and social consequences caused by drug prohibition similar? I hope that I can answer this question in the next chapters.

VICTIMS AND CASUALTIES

The Downtown Eastside (DTES) section of Vancouver, British Columbia, Canada, shares many similarities with any inner city around the world. Its social characteristics are comprised of a class of individuals who for one reason or another share a commonality with the rest. There are the working poor, the unemployed, the underemployed, the non-employable, the mentally ill, the medically ill, the social victims (drug addicts), the social predators (drug dealers), the prostitutes (victims) etc. Visual minorities and ethnic groups may choose to reside in this inner city setting because of economics. The cost of living is relatively less than the cost of middle class neighbourhoods like North Vancouver, West Vancouver and so on.

Similar to any other city, DTES has its administrative body comprised of social workers, by-law regulators, uniformed police, and the drug squad law enforcement, whose main task is to enforce drug prohibition, as it is defined by federal and provincial laws. There are women's and men's shelters, run-down hotels, room rental housing, small grocery stores, pawn shops, run-down stores, cheap cafes, run-down buildings, an odd bank here and there, social associations made up of government employees and volunteers, religious groups who feed the poor **after** they hear religious sermons, walk-in clinics, counsellors and volunteers, police stations and so on. When you look closely at this social environment, you notice that it is comprised of intended and un-intended casualties and by intended and unintended beneficiaries of such a social setting. More later.

There are no classical economic activities within the social boundaries of this community. There are no productive forces, no classical business activities that generate income and consumer input and output. Those individuals who hold local regular work are there only during their working hours. Their contribution to this socio-economic environment is minimal, at best. Their economic power is utilized in the communities where they reside, where their families are provided for where their children grow up and where they attend schools. In fact, their very own income derives from outside, and not because of their own initiatives. Their sense of humanism, for the well being of the community, is felt and given in a bureaucratic manner. What makes this a classical cultural segregation is that it is essentially distinct from the rest of society. Its human character is made of delusional hope, despair, self-delusion, altruism (voluntarism), and a balance of self-destruction and self-preservation (the latter, to a lesser degree). There is a sense of unity and social identity among the residents, whose lives are guided by the next score, the next fix or the next step to initiate the same process. As victims of drug prohibition, their most important singular task of survival is finding what is prohibited to them: illegal drugs. This is the central core of their daily focus. It is the axis regarding their purpose in life, their being of existence. It is a medical condition called addiction. It can be caused by *addictive* drugs, regardless of their marketing classification of being "legal" or "illegal". In other words, drug addiction is neither a criminal condition nor is it a moral failure. It is what it is, a physical functioning of *somatic* and *mental* complications.

A large part of the human environment on "skid row" are the homeless "residents" who occupy every possible structural cranny including doorways, alleys, abandoned garbage dumps, street benches, cardboard, sleeping bags and tents. Who are these people, and where do they come from? The short answer is that their origin is of no consequence. But it is reasonable to conclude that "they" have all come from somewhere else.

Whatever human condition 'skidded' them through and led them here, this was their final destination/arrival point. They arrived here by every means which was imposed upon them: poverty, the prison system, a lack of education, making wrong choices, family tragedy, emotional post-traumatic disorder, the boom and bust economy, the financial ruins of long-lasting drug addiction etc. Their social "cousins" are those who can still afford to pay for their drug use, and who remain free from the skid row slide. They are teens from all walks of life, businessmen, blue-collar workers, white collar workers, financiers (who need a fix to wind down from their daily stress), politicians, "pseudo-moralists" of the Right, Left-leaning intellectuals, and the list goes on. Most people think that drug addicts and recreational users are "they", who exist in a void, and that it has little or nothing to do with members of your or my family. Is it possible that one or more of those individuals may be your child, your sister, brother, husband, wife, father or mother? My point is that there is a superficial metaphorical wall that separates skid row from the recreational users and drug addicts. Don't be swayed by their appearance, or their dreadful situation, whether they reside on skid-row or are its possible future inhabitants. Their present combined widespread use of drugs–measured in economic value–is immense !

During any prohibition there are forces that are an integral part of its implementation and functioning. All forces that operate under prohibition are the essential products of the prohibition. They are *real* functional forces, not a product of someone's imagination and/or moral and conspiratorial theory. It has to do with the realism of prohibition; that is, how it operates within opposing confrontational forces, i.e. the illegal drug trade, vs. the operational services of prohibition. The social and economic value of the recreational or addictive drug users is that on the one hand, they are all consumers and the marketing base of the illegal drug trade. On the other hand, they are equally client recipients of the prohibition service industry.

One of the "players" in the prohibition arena is the large scale illegal drug dealer. Another is the micro-dealer of drugs. Below them are the street level drug-vendors whom one can find in certain neighbourhoods, nightclubs, colleges, universities and on skid-row. After more than nine decades of drug prohibition, large-scale drug dealers have had the time to get organized into cartels, mafia, families, motorcycle gangs or small groups of independent operators not yet integrated with organized crime. Those large scale drug dealers can be smugglers or only distributors. They are groups of individuals who are guided by greed, a sense of power and the need to be feared by their underlings. They are both astute and ruthless, and they are the ultimate by-product of drug prohibition. Some of them are brave enough to kill others but too cowardly to die in jail, so they become informers against their own kind. They deal in smuggling marijuana, heroin, cocaine, amphetamines and other drugs. Their drugs are unadulterated (90% or 100% purity). They supply a large number of sub-drug dealers (wholesalers) who redistribute to their contacts, the micro-drug dealers.

Micro-drug dealers are a separate class unto themselves. They are the frontline of the illicit drug trade. Whether they are dealing on behalf of organized crime or as independent agents, they are the people who are targeted by the law enforcement of prohibition. They supply the street-level drug dealers, from street gangs to the social groups of professionals, businessmen, bars and nightclub owners and their clientele, the "beautiful people" of arts and music, teens and college students. At the time of this writing, my sixty-eight year old neighbour is getting her supply of marijuana from her long time dealer. At the bottom of the scale are the skid row dealers who are part of the local drug scene and generally are drug addicts themselves. For these people, selling is not motivated by greed for money and power. Rather, it is a lifestyle of drug abuse and a means to finance their own addiction. Because of the concentration of the drug population on skid row, outside drug suppliers, drug squad law enforcement, informers, prostitutes desperate to earn enough for a fix, transients from across the country, newly paroled prisoners, the homeless, boosters selling their stolen goods, all form a cultural phenomenon unlike any other sector of our society. All are living fearfully, under the shadow of drug prohibition.

The micro-market of illicit narcotics is not very visible, since the drug being transported, stored and sold, at street level, are not bulky. Some street vendors hide their heroin capsules inside rubber balloons or "bundles" attached to a string. They are swallowed for safekeeping and thus are out of sight. The heroin capsules will be retrieved and sold when needed. When a member of the drug squad arrests a street vendor, the first place they forcefully check is his or her mouth, before the vendor swallows the string with the attached bundle of drugs. Other orifices are also used for hiding, transporting and retrieving drugs as needed.

The prohibition of drugs has caused a tremendous health problem for the recipients of illegal drugs. In the secretive world of producing, smuggling, cutting, distributing and adulterating narcotics, quality control is of the least importance. The health of those involved in the contraband trade is not affected by the contaminants contained in their illicit drugs. What is important for illegal traders is the speed by which they can pass on their drugs to the next level of distribution. Prohibition is a permanent "state of siege" against drug trafficking. Therefore, traffickers need to reduce the level of siege by moving their drugs as quickly as possible. Health issues are not part of the mentality of drug traffickers. Their concern is to utilize what dilutes illicit drugs most easily, is least expensive, easy to obtain, and with relatively non-toxic side-effects. Most overdose deaths are caused when drug users have lost their tolerance to the toxicity found in the impurities of the cutting agents. By the time the heroin or cocaine arrives at the inner-city street level, the local drug vendor will be the first to try the potency of the drug. He or she will then keep some of this for his own use. He will then "adjust" the potency of the remaining drug with a cutting agent of his/her choice to increase the volume and thus cover the cost of his own drug use.

The human tragedy under the state of siege of drug prohibition extends to the health problems of the drug addicts. Homelessness, mental problems, poverty, lack of proper bodily hygiene, lack of proper nutrition, and entrapment in an inhuman environment where compassion is only a bureaucratic task, multiplies health problems tenfold. I am referring to IDUs. Injection Drug Users account for more than 60% of all new Hepatitis C virus (HCV)cases in the United States. Studies show that 58% of new IDUs are infected within six to eight months of *initial* injection. Think about this for a moment. Due to lack of a clinical supply of sterilized injection needles, cotton, cookers and water, newcomers into the injection drug scene are forced to use whatever is available to them. This means they will share with other drug addicts previously used needles and paraphernalia with a high probability of being infected with HCV, HIV and AIDS. The cost of sterilized paraphernalia is just a few cents per day. On the other hand, the cost over a lifetime of HCV, HIV and AIDS may accumulate into hundreds of thousands of dollars per infected drug addict. Besides, at the moment there is no vaccine against HCV available, thus, whatever treatment is provided to the HCV victim is ineffective and financially wasteful. Sterilized drug paraphernalia available through "shooting galleries" prevent the transmission of disease in the immediate areas where those are located. The shooting galleries are useful solely because of the concentration of a large drug addict population. But the majority of injection drug users are not located in a single location. This means that an injection drug addict spends a large part of his day looking to score money to pay for his injection. When he finds the money, he then has to travel to where his supplier is located to purchase his drug. When he finally scores his drug, the only thought in his mind is the cooking and injection of the drug. If he is near a shooting gallery, he most likely will go there to receive his sterilized drug paraphernalia. However, because he is very anxious to inject now, he will not take the time to travel very far to a shooting gallery. Instead, he will use any syringe and cooker available, regardless of if it had been used previously by another drug addict. You see, most heavily addicted drug addicts travel great distances (within the city) looking for a score, or a "John" to pay for sex, or to sell whatever drug he/she has available. Being heavily opiated in heroin does not make him/her *up to par* for dealing in drugs on the street.

This is a classical case of prohibition, the way in which all illegal products sold drugs, alcohol, tobacco, food etc.–are diluted and adulterated at each link on the distribution chain. Depending upon the strength of their purity, most prohibited products are adulterated to some degree or another. It happened during the Alcohol Prohibition of the 1920's where moonshine of suspicious quality was used as an adulterant mixed into smuggled liquor from Canada and the Caribbean. It happened during the Peruvian prohibition on the importation of goods and services during early 1990's, where most alcoholic beverages were diluted with industrial alcohol. Within prohibition are the cultural roots of criminality, which brings out the worst of human nature, all in the name of greed. Nothing, absolutely nothing, can prevent or reduce the harm that drug prohibition causes upon the most vulnerable adult populations of our society: the mentally ill, the chemically addicted, the homeless and the socially disoriented. We are collectively guilty of preying upon the meek, by charging, prosecuting, and imprisoning them, and also by exposing them to incurable diseases, under the guise of a misplaced "civilized" moralism and false humanism. I'll explain.

Essential to the temperance/prohibition movement is the war on drugs. Enforcers of temperance/prohibition are the frontline drug warriors and advocates of *abstinence* or *harm reduction* personnel. Drug warriors are comprised of the law enforcement *drug squads* and their *informers*. These bodies are supported by the legal system of prohibition on both federal and state or provincial levels. Non-law enforcement (abstinence and harm reduction) persons are essentially comprised of social workers, medical staff, counsellors and religious volunteers. All of the above share a singular goal: the *control* of drug use/abuse. For example, *abstinence* advocators are members of Drug Anonymous, Alcoholic Anonymous, the Salvation Army and so on. The h*arm reductionists* social organizations advocate syringe exchange programs, the establishment of "shooting-galleries", methods of controlling harm addiction, health prevention programs, etc. All of the above are organizational bodies with their own supporters, operating facilities, budgets, trained personnel and designated goals.

At the law and order level, I maintain that the combination of drug prohibition and repression promotes widespread major and petty crime. As far as law enforcement and major criminal activities are concerned, large and small-scale drug trafficking is the (objective) ally of drug prohibition. Both are mutually inclusive natural opposites that ensure drug trafficking and organizational repression take place equally. This threatens the public's safety, personal freedoms and human rights. As for petty crime, drug prohibition is the driving force behind many crimes and offences, such as burglaries, shoplifting, robberies, hold-ups, purse snatching, car thefts, breaking into pharmacies, prostitution, and other crimes against people and property. Large-scale drug trafficking requires an equally large organizational force to counter it. This includes extensive surveillance technology and trained personnel, well placed and paid informers, arms and equipment, central operational facilities, and all around logistical capabilities. As in any type of organization, the extension or reduction of its size depends upon its operational scope. This operational scope and designated goal is none other than the War on Drugs.

As the main combatant force implementing anti-drug policy, its aim is to control not only the illicit supply of drugs, but also the public's demand, especially among the young, and both white and blue collar workers. It must be pointed out that <u>no strategy</u> <u>explicitly exists aimed solely at the total elimination of drug</u> <u>trafficking</u> ! Instead, drug strategy aims to reduce the supply of drugs through major drug trafficking and micro-narcotic dealings. Secondary in the scale of priorities is the reduction of the demand for drugs through joint drug prevention programs. This includes awareness initiatives for the young and the general public, as well as assisting in the reduction of harm and spread of drug related illnesses. The latter concept of harm reduction often conveys different meaning. For drug enforcement personnel, it means *total abstinence,* while harm reductionists aim to help divert drug users from their addiction.

The enforcers of drug prohibition clearly rely on street informers recruited to provide information against other drug dealers so they can obtain evidence leading to drug-related prosecutions. Some are paid informers while others are "paid" by different means. In the murky world of drug trafficking, full of mistrust and deceit, everyone has his/her price. Anyone who is familiar with contraband, bootlegging and drug trafficking would be aware that the drug scene is full of treachery. There are more informers in the drug trade than in any other area of crime. Often, false information is given by informers who are facing prosecution for drug offences. In other words, those informers have far more complex motives for giving information against others in return for a lighter sentence than the paid informers who give information in return for a fee. Some micro-drug dealers are "let" to operate freely–that is, against the law–and are protected against possible arrests. This is typical drug squad mentality, which operates under the assumption of *"Let one bird go, to catch the rest"*. Others who are in a "hook" of legal jeopardy are extorted by law enforcement officers and used to inform against other drug dealers.

This is a formal component of law enforcement strategy to entice, threaten and manipulate drug addicts to inform on others. The police attitude towards common drug addicts is one which says it all, for "they are the scourge of the earth," not deserving any human consideration. This attitude, of course, is hidden from the general public, unless someone's child has been a victim of police undercover brutality. I do not say this lightly, for I had an active part in breaking the prohibition laws. Although I have never been part of the drug scene, I still shared the same "playground". I have seen the inhumanity and brutality by those on both sides of the law, their mutual hostility, deception and victimization. The fact that one side has a uniform does not justify its abuse and imposition of extra-legal enforcement against drug addicts. I have great respect for those police officers who are brave enough to speak out and be members of the *Law Enforcement Against Drug Prohibition.* For those officers, and for me, the issue of drug prohibition is not an academic exercise. It has to do with preventing the further dehumanization of demoralized youth, the vulnerable, the sick and the victims of the power struggle between opposing organized hostile forces. Drug addicts are already victims of their illness. How could the twisted logic of prohibition ever alleviate their pain and help them? Does the current "patch work" called Harm Reduction go beyond attempting to control the spread of diseases caused by drug injection? What is Harm Reduction but the *public relations* social mask of the prohibition's War on Drugs?

Those groups and individuals who advocate harm reduction programs need to realize that their ideas are part of the long established "positive" side of temperance drug prohibition. It is because temperance public outreach still continues as it was originally thought of: a) outlawing drug sales, b) total abstinence and c) harm reduction of illicit drugs/alcohol. Adapting their stance of harm reduction alone further prolongs the War on Drugs. Reading this, you may raise your eyebrows because the field workers are altruistic. Their altruistic ideas of harm reduction are clouded by their sentiment, not by the realism of reduction. As far back as 1910, in the US, treatment programs for drug users were implemented for a long period.

Although some users benefit from treatment, most relapse after successful treatments. This holds true even today. Improving programs, needle exchange and the use of sterilized paraphernalia does help, but it still does not lead to a high success rate against drug abuse. Only a certain percentage of drug addicts can terminate their drug addiction through their own efforts. True enough, some 25% of drug addicts stopped their drug use through natural-recovery. What can be done for other 75%? A temperance solution is to introduce them to an active program to further prevent health damage through harm reduction interventions.

On the other hand, imprisoning drug addicts is not a preventative program, because drugs are available in prisons. The problem of drug use is prevalent in local communities. Inner-city residents including those of Vancouver's Downtown East Side, are upset by the growing size and increasingly blatant character of the growing illicit drug market. Buyers and sellers conduct their trade nearly openly. There is little regard for the impact of their activities on the community. People's fear of crime is real. The presence of the drug market symbolizes prohibition's inability to maintain public order. Simply put, it is not possible to arrest every buyer and seller, and there is not enough room in the prison system to "warehouse" every offender. The prison system does not have the capacity to maintain the thousands of low-level drug offenders. The question is, other than the temperance hit and miss patchwork, is it possible to terminate *most* drug use in prisons, schools and the workplace in an open society? This is a realistic question, one of open-mindedness and pragmatism. Do harm reduction programs, at any level, reduce the abuse of drugs?

Advocates of drug prohibition argue that particular drugs must be declared illegal because they are harmful. That illegal drugs are, by their chemical properties, harmful substances is attested to by the growing harm reduction movement. A reluctant ally of the harm reduction movement is the US Drug Enforcement

Administration. It does not see harm reduction as a threat to its present *status quo* of drug prohibition. The DEA's "stick" is not at all diminished by harm reduction's "carrot" approach to alleviate and reduce drug related diseases. Aside from the partial reduction of drug-related diseases, the harm reductionists remind us that the cost of drug user rehabilitation is far lower than the cost of imprisonment. But harm reductionists remain silent in regards to the health harms of illicit drugs caused by the lack of legal regulation of its purity, contamination level and strength. The DEA's war on drugs "stick" is justified by its incoherent claim that,

"Crime, violence and drug use go hand in hand. Six times as many homicides are committed by people under the influence of drugs, as by those who are looking for money to buy drugs. Most drug crimes aren't committed by people trying to pay for drugs, they're committed by people on drugs".

(US DEA (2003) "Speaking Out Against Drug Legislation")

The reason whether a drug buyer or a drug-user has committed a violent crime is of no consequence, for a drug-related crime is a drug-related crime. The **more** people that are addicted to hard drugs, the **more** likely they'll commit a crime. The **fewer** people addicted to hard drugs the **fewer** crimes will be committed. The legalization of drugs, therefore, will reduce the likelihood of people's drug addiction and thus, the reduction of drug-related crimes for both the drug buyers and the drug users. Because the DEA's attention is directed towards the drug users, the harm reduction programs fit well with the prevention and rehabilitation of drug use. This reluctant alliance between drug law enforcement and harm reductionists was not created under some kind of conspiracy. It is the natural unity of two opposites: the "stick" is <u>negative</u>, the "carrot" is <u>positive</u>–one is the natural extension of the other. As independent as they may appear to be from each other, both have an institutional interest in maintaining the present status quo. Prohibition's present high volume of drug addiction, with its allocation of vast sums of money to law enforcement, diminishes the funds available for drug education, treatment, harm reduction facilities and preventative social programs (needle exchange). It is because of this that only a handful of public drug facilities were created, and some of those are threatened by the legal actions of right-wing federal political leaders. The right-wing Conservative government will take legal action against the Vancouver's InSide needle-exchange program. In the US, low-income men and especially pregnant women who abuse drugs often have no medical insurance or Medicaid to pay for drug addiction treatment. Instead, federal and state governments prosecute and imprison these women without regard to the health of both mothers and their children. Prohibition's war on drugs has failed to reduce, curb or eliminate the harmful use of illicit drugs. Instead, it has created other serious social problems. The militarization of drug law enforcement has also created violent conflicts, disproportionately so in poor inner cities. This irrational act has turned poor neighbourhoods into war zones and their residents are prohibition's primary war casualties.

Pragmatic realism and rational thinking shows that drugs are here to stay. The slogan of "Not Drug Free - Just Less Free" is advocated by fence-sitters who refuse to think 'outside the box' (the use of metaphors sometimes helps). Throughout human history (see chronology) humans have used drugs for recreational, medicinal or religious reasons to alter consciousness. For whatever reasons, it is a basic human habit to seek psychoactive drugs. In the highlands of Peru, indigenous men and women, (and I did as well), take coca leaf breaks–boiled as tea–the way others use coffee or tea breaks. I have never gotten "high" drinking coca tea. In North America, tobacco and peyote have been used for religious reasons as Europeans have used wine or as some Muslim countries have tolerated the use of opium or hashish. A "not drug free - just less free" approach to a drug solution is not a realistic social goal. Nor is it realistic to criminalize drug use, and to surrender all control of potentially dangerous drugs to organized criminal gangs who care less about the addicts' health than about making a lot of money.

True enough, it is not possible to predict how drug use patterns would change under a system of regulated manufacture, distribution and sale of currently illegal drugs. From my experience within the prohibition scene for more than five years, I can confirm this: a) that under the iron rules of prohibition, it is the producers and distributors and **not** the consumers who control the market and b) that prohibition fosters the production of adulterated products and the sale/distribution of these uncontrolled and unmeasured drugs. Adulterated alcoholic products and chemically-cut agents mixed with drugs are primary examples. I can also confirm that prohibition is the natural partner and creator of organized crime; for without prohibition, there would be no criminal drug elements benefiting from the current situation. What are the current forces that make up the structural elements of prohibition? Who benefits from it?

❖ The temperance movement

❖ The religious moralists

❖ The political opportunists

❖ The Drug Law Enforcement's Budget Office(DEA)

❖ The State Law Enforcement Budget Office

❖ Both Federal and State Prison Systems

❖ Both Federal and State Parole Systems

❖ The Federal and State Judges and Prosecutors

- ❖ Judicial Courts, their Clerks, Secretaries etc

- ❖ The Clerical staff of the Justice Department

- ❖ The Trial Lawyers (paid) and their personnel

- ❖ The Public Defenders and their personnel

- ❖ The paid drug informers

- ❖ The producers of illicit drugs

- ❖ The Smugglers/Distributors of Illicit Drugs

- ❖ Organized Crime groups, Mafia, motorcycle gangs

- ❖ Middle level drug traffickers

- ❖ Street level drug traffickers

- ❖ Groups operating public sponsored Harm-Reduction programs, their paid staff and facilities

- ❖ The "shooting-galleries" needle-exchange/sterilized Paraphernalia programs, nurses and counsellors

- ❖ Social workers related to the drug addiction crisis

- ❖ Publicly funded clinical drug treatment facilities

- ❖ Privately funded drug detoxification treatments

- ❖ Private/public funded psychological treatments

- ❖ Publishers of Self-help books on drug treatment

I need to state clearly that I am not a conspiratorial theorist speculating on the "unity" of these circumstantial partners. I am simply presenting a concrete list of willing or unwilling beneficiaries whose mutual existence depends upon continued prohibition. There is no doubt in my mind that a lot of the groups and persons involved in the above list have altruistic intentions in their hearts. Most believe that their work truly helps the "unfortunate". I have also talked with individuals who view their work with the drug addiction programs as temporary action until "something better" comes along.

There are a number of scientific and academic theories offering something better to counter the "drug problem," including how to minimize drug addiction, hospitalization, and imprisonment through community work, arguments for or against simple drug-possession, partial legalization, acupuncture, religion and spiritualism, and schools self-esteem and extra-curriculum programs etc. After one hundred years of legalized drug prohibition, experience shows that the militarization of the War on Drugs, and the criminalization of drugs has not curbed or eliminated drug-related crimes. The "noble experiment" has totally failed ! The good intentions of harm reduction programs are, at best, a social patchwork until something better comes along. Intentionally or unintentionally, their vested interests lie with the continuation of drug prohibition. The termination of prohibition would also mean the termination of their comfortable salaries, their families' futures, their pension plans, their professional advancement, their organizational budgets, and their political and judicial careers. It is said that one's view of the world is shaped by one's professional occupation. Again, I want to emphasize to you, that there are no backroom conspirators whose master plan it is to ensure the continuation of drug prohibition. What I am saying, however, is that the majority of people will **not** "bite the hand that feeds them." In order to avoid looking at related issues deeper, an official will tend to declare that, " I am just doing my job the best I can." Prohibition is about conformity, an unchallenged style of life imposed upon you by your "betters" who know what is best for you. The legalization of drugs is not about the legalization of criminality. The legalization of drugs is about eliminating crimes related to the illicit production, distribution and sale of contaminated drugs. It is about protecting our youth, the sick and the meek. It is about eliminating billions of wasteful dollars spent on drug prohibition, eliminating the human tragedy caused by imprisonment, ending discrimination against visual minorities, ending militarized solutions to the medical problems caused by drug addiction, ending the drug related violent crimes of drug trafficking and simple drug possession, and reducing crimes against people and property. We have become a nation of jailers and a dysfunctional institutional wasteland. We have turned a social administrative entity called society into a labyrinth of legalisms. The irony is that we are being told that we are free! But, that's another subject.

9

WAR ON DRUGS:
AN ANATOMY OF FAILURE

All War is Based on Deception

"The Art of War" by Sun Tzu, circa 500 B.C.

This is a story of how the War on Drugs turned into one of the most sustaining and costly defeats that the most powerful country on earth, sensing a piñata full of drugs, swung to hit and missed. It is a story of drug warriors on both sides of the law, countless deaths on each side, followed by the end of one battle against drugs and the beginning of another.

The offences of drug use and abuse were once a simple police matter; an offender was captured, tried and sentenced to jail. The whole drug law enforcement process was part of normal police work, no more nor less than any other crime. The transformation from "gum-shoe" police work to the war on drugs, however, began following the 1961 UN Convention and accelerated during the Nixon Administration. For those Republican politicians in Washington, the problem of drugs was regarded as a failure of America's temperance morality. Not far from this, the military brass and politicians were receiving reports that returning soldiers from Vietnam were hooked on heroin and marijuana. The panic many Americans felt about the anti-war demonstrations, the marijuana smoking hippies, crime and social unrest became "evidence" of drug abuse. This was not a mere assumption on the part of the politicians and the military, for Nixon truly believed that drugs were the cause of social unrest. The Nixonian solution to drug use was twofold: the restoration of the temperance morality, and the law and order battle against drugs. He appointed Governor Shafer to find evidence/solution to the drug problem. The "Shafer Commission" presented an honest conclusion and reported back that marijuana should no longer be a criminal offence. Needless to say, the conclusion of the Blue Ribbon Report freaked out Nixon who yelled, "We need, and I use the word 'all-out war', on all fronts..." This "all out war" caused hundreds of thousands of arrests for marijuana possession alone. I remember a case in Texas, where a man was sentenced to 10 years in prison for possession of 1 single joint of marijuana.

The Nixon White House tapes from 1971-1972 clearly demonstrate that the current war on drugs is the result of twisted Nixonian prejudice and cultural bigotry. Nixon wanted a report which supported his views, "law and order" and "tough on crime" policies, no matter what the Shafer Report evidence presented. Nixon blamed calls for marijuana legalization on Jews, homosexuals, communists and on people's moral failure. When the conservative administration decided how to handle marijuana possession, Nixon's Christian temperance prejudices did more to dominate the desired course than the rational approach of the Shafer Commission. Had Nixon followed the advice of the Governor's recommendations, rather than his own biases, "gum-shoe" police work would have continued. American taxpayers would have spent a lot less on law enforcement and a million less people would have been arrested. It is estimated that since 1973, more than 15 million people have been arrested on marijuana charges alone. Nixon's Christian bigotry against the "others" is a common religious phenomenon. During his term as President of the United States, he commissioned an investigation to see how many Jews were employed in the White House. His views were clear to his class of people who used "others" as scapegoats:

"I see another thing in the news summary this morning about it. That's a funny thing, everyone of these bastards that are out for the legalizing of marijuana is Jewish. What the Christ is the matter with the Jews, what is the matter with them." I suppose its because most of them are psychiatrists..."

"...You see, homosexuality, dope, immorality in general. These are the enemies of strong societies. That's why the Communists and the left-wingers are pushing the stuff [drugs], they're trying to destroy us"

..."Enforce the law, [we] got to scare them."

In 1973, Nixon gave the job of " got to scare them" to the newly formed Drug Enforcement Administration (DEA). Calling narcotics "public enemy number one in the United States", he escalated the war on drugs against users and producers from around the world. The DEA is not a police force, nor can it be considered a law enforcement agency in a strict legal sense. From its inception, DEA had a clear mission, that is, its "war-mentality" is geared toward declaring a war and enforcing a political policy, not a law. Its "war-mentality" was set by Nixon's directive of "we got to scare them", and "them" were the 1960's alienated youth and the visual minorities who were the main body of recreational drug users. This war has now evolved into a cultural war against Americans, and escalated into the killing-fields of Mexico, Colombia, Peru, Bolivia, and the rest of Latin America and Asia. Declaring a war tends to arm the conflicting participants on both sides of the conflict. The DEA is a well armed militaristic force, and so are the opponents in the drug trade. The DEA maintains 21 domestic divisions with 227 field offices. Although its original mandate was to enforce drug laws in the United States, it has 86 foreign offices in 62 countries with an annual budget of 2.451 billion dollars (2005 estimates). It employs 11,000 people, including over 5,500 field agents who direct or conduct the war on drugs. It has its own Aviation Division with 106 aircrafts and 124 DEA pilots. It began its undeclared war against the lifestyle of American youths in the 1960's; it has evolved today into a full-scale cultural war against anyone using or producing, marijuana or psychedelic drugs.

Little has been reported on how coca producing countries react to the presence of the DEA within their borders. The internalization of the DEA's drug enforcement agencies around the world is expressed by its application of US foreign policy in other countries. This hegemonic behaviour explains how and why an American drug enforcement agency has become a powerful presence in the Americas and a source of bitter resentment in the last decades. US anti-drug agents have reached outside US borders with the primary objective of enforcing American laws more effectively. They have aggressively travelled abroad and established DEA subsidiaries in other countries, making clear that the international drug trade is from now on illegal under US drug laws. This has meant crossing the borders in hot pursuit of drug dealers or demanding that the DEA local counterpart agency of another country participate in anti-drug enforcement or intelligence gathering missions. Bolivia frequently has expressed that drug-related transgressions of its territorial sovereignty comes from DEA attempts to enforce United States drug laws.

Through the corruption of local army and war lords around the world, the DEA has behaved like an extra-sovereign power with no regards to cultural customs or civil and human rights. In fact, the main source of anti-American sentiment in Latin America stems from the DEA's arrogance expressed by its hegemonic power. I have seen the DEA's paid mercenaries in their killing fields of Peru and in the jungles of Bolivia. I have heard their drunken-sick laughter when describing their notorious acts against the coca campesinos whom they regard as sub-humans. I have looked into their lifeless eyes for any sense of human remorse. I never noticed any. Their "heroic" acts, as described by their DEA master policy makers, is for public consumption and for the dysfunctional religious "law and order" minds back home. In the coca regions of Southern Colombia, in the Upper Huallaga Valley of Peru and in the Chapare and Yungas regions of Bolivia, more than coca leaves is being eradicated by the DEA's paid aerial fumigation. The chemical spraying of thousands of acres of coca has also destroyed the food crops of the already impoverished indigenous people. Chemical fumigation has also affected the health of indigenous women and children, who have no other choice but to continue living in the same contaminated environment. This herbicidal warfare program appears to be similar to the Orange Agent defoliant program during the

Vietnam War. The chemical dioxins–an environmental pollutant–has exposed millions of people to health problems. Large areas of the jungle rainforest have been destroyed, along with family vegetable patches and livestock. The DEA's Vietnam-era helicopters upload their drug agents who are accompanied by paid mercenaries in "search and destroy" missions of primitive cocaine "kitchens" concealed in the surrounding jungle. Dressed in battle fatigues and armed with AR15 assault rifles, they carry out dozens of carnage missions against hostile peasants. Murdering and destroying in the jungles of Peru, Bolivia and Colombia is not exactly front page news. The deaths of *campesinos* is not a worthwhile story. I have shared coca tea with a group of jungle mercenaries while traveling (looking for gold) in the jungle of Bolivia. They were part of road control units, checking vehicles for hidden *pasta de coca intended* for local consumption or for the labs to be converted into pure cocaine. The irony is that the same mercs, with their cheeks packed with coca leaves, planned the eradication of the same coca plants they were enjoying. I was also ensured by friends in the Chapare region that most of the DEA agents and their mercenaries were also cocaine users. The chemical eradication of coca plants has been contaminating rivers and streams which, further downstream, are the only water sources for rural peasants and indigenous tribes not involved themselves in coca cultivation.

Those illegal operations have been going on in South America for the last 30 years. Yet, the DEA has failed to achieve any of its stated objectives and failed to dramatically curtail the flow of drugs into the US. Latest reports show that the DEA has seized a reported $1.4 billion in illegal drug trade earnings and $478 million (valued at street level) worth of illegal drugs. How does this compare with the DEA's annual budget of more than 2 billion dollars? According to the White House Office of Drug Control Policy, the sum total of the world's drugs sold in the United States is as much as $66 billion dollars a year, making the DEA's seizures dismal. It is less than 1% effective against the 66 billion dollars involved in the drug trade. The "law and order" defenders of the DEA's anti-drug record argue that the agency has a positive effect beyond its relatively dismal annual drug seizures. They claim the agency is placing pressure on drug traffickers, which causes the raising of prices for consumers. However, this "pressure on drug traffickers" does not reduce the affordability of drugs; it simply forces drug addicts to commit more crimes in order to support their addiction. The DEA's eradication programs are driven by the theory that decreasing coca production will make cocaine scarce and more expensive, thereby decreasing into its use. Such an idiotic theory is part of the anatomy of failure, which must have been conceived by a bureaucrat desk-warrior with no field experience. Reality, however, has proven this theory to be wishful thinking. First, anyone who has travelled in the jungles of Peru and Bolivia coca cultivation areas can witness this: when an eradication scheme succeeds in reducing coca cultivation in one area, other cocaleros whose plantations survive eradication earn more money for their coca. Secondly, a shortage of coca leaf supplies entices other coca farmers to move into or expand coca cultivation. This is the basic free market principle of supply and demand, which the DEA bureaucrats have forgotten to remember from #101 Economics. Thirdly, eradications entice coca growers to harvest coca more carefully, and process coca leaves longer to extract more pasta de coca. Fourth, cocaleros are born in the jungle, know it well, and thus they will then cultivate coca in less accessible plots that are deeper in the jungle. Fifth, the more that eradication has been conducted in Peru, Bolivia, Argentina, Chile and Colombia, the more that cocaine cultivation has skyrocketed in Mexico and other parts of Central America. Lastly, the DEA's manual and chemical eradication methods with herbicides are perceived by the cocaleros as acts, not only of biochemical warfare, but of "cultural imperialism" to eliminate the benign culture of coca use as well.

Air transportation is the most convenient, timely and cost effective means of shipping cocaine base via Peru, Ecuador and Bolivia to the Colombian cocaine producing labs. A small percentage of shipping cocaine base is done by river, because the Amazonian river systems in the Peru-Colombia border region flows primarily west to east. River shipments, however, take a lot longer to complete and run a greater risk of cargo loss due to competing nacro-cartels, river bandits, drug patrol enforcement agencies, spoilage or geographical difficulties. Thus, shipping methods vary depending on the circumstances and the level of anti-drug operations in a given area. The DEA believes that 90% of Peruvian cocaine base is flown directly to Colombia via small civil navigation airplanes. Those small airplanes illegally enter Peru airspace by run-around routes and in jungle strips, where bundles of cocaine base are immediately loaded onto the plane. The normal turnaround time is as swift as 5 minutes. The pilots typically time the flights to avoid routes that transit areas where air traffic control can detect their movements. Near the air-strips are hidden warehouses to store cocaine-base and fuel tanks for refuelling the planes. These airstrips are within the private properties of local businessmen who receive between $3.000 to $5.000 per airplane landing. One of these was an unassuming man named "El Vaticano" who, I once met briefly. His private property was located next to an army base. This, however, did not prevent "El Vaticano" from doing business with drug traffickers, for he simply shared his profits with the army brass. Too bad for "El Vaticano", for when the "crap hit the fan", and the army looked for a scapegoat, they arrested him and eventually he was sentenced to life in prison without the chance of parole. The last time I heard of "El Vaticano", he was in the naval base of Callao, Lima, in an below-ground level prison, next to Abimael Guzman, leader of the Sandero Luminoso rebel group.

Furthermore, because of the vastness of the coca cultivation area in the Brazilian Amazonian, Peruvian and Bolivian jungles, the traffickers always found loopholes that allowed them to continue their illicit aircraft and river shipments of drugs. True enough, when one flies over the Upper Huallaga Valley coca cultivation region, one can see in the green landscape below the distinct shapes of small planes that have been shot down or crash-landed to avoid arrest. Still, there are several airfields in western Peru which continue to support flights via Ecuador to Colombia, while the river networks provide a means to transport precursor chemicals from Brazil to cocaine processing in Bolivia and Peru.

In the last few years, drug traffickers have begun to use Brazil's vast Amazonian region to avoid the DEA's sponsored anti-drug operations. Brazilian participation in the drug transportation industry is also a big business to the local communities. A side effect of the drug traffickers using Brazilian airspace is the Brazilian aero-taxis [bush-pilots]. Companies and farmers who owned small civil aviation airplanes have became more interested in the quick profits available through drug transportation as "part-time" contractors. Soya-bean farmers and cattle ranchers are increasingly penetrating the Amazonian region in order to enlarge their land holdings. Their geographical isolation provides drug trade routes not yet charted by the Brazilian DEA forces. Signs indicate that the growing of coca plants is increasing. Crop seizures and drug trafficking are on the rise in Ecuador, a spill-over from Peru and Colombia. Could Ecuador become a major coca-growing country like its neighbours Colombia to the north, and Peru to the south? Ecuadorian and US DEA anti-narcotics agents in this Andean country report a rise of illegal coca crops along its northern border with Colombia. It was the infamous drug trafficker Pablo Escobar who first began transporting coca from Ecuador, long before large-scale coca cultivation came to Colombia. The narco-cartels see Ecuador and its maritime territory as an opportunity to realize their trafficking. The northern province of Esmeraldas borders on the Colombian state of Nariño, providing an ideal ground for coca-farming and coca processing. As the pressure on the drug trade from paramilitary, left-wing rebels and anti-drug agencies increases in Colombia, Ecuador has taken on a bigger role as a global transit channel from Colombian and Peruvian cocaine trafficking. The river networks in the mineral rich Peruvian border territory, along with the jungle density, makes controlling illicit trafficking of both incoming chemicals and outgoing cocaine base, nearly impossible. River patrols, conducted by Peruvian and Ecuadorian special forces are a common sight and are of little threat to drug traffickers who share a common knowledge of the terrain.

This is a "cat and mouse", "hide and seek" or "search and destroy" conflict between drug traffickers and the DEA forces. The northern border region has long suffered from spill-over of the Colombian conflict, including increased violence, a steady flow of refugees and environmental and health impacts from chemical fumigation just over the Ecuadorian border. The present day government has renewed efforts to force the DEA to cease aerial spraying along its northern border. Until 2009, the US military base in Manta was apparently used for counter-drug surveillance numbering 100 flights per month. One long-standing concern is that the DEA's intelligence surveillance gathering is being used to support not only its anti-drug operations, but the US's counter-insurgency strategy in Colombia. Hence, the DEA has violated its own legal mandate by involving Ecuador directly in Colombian's internal conflict. While such forms of US-DEA intervention may have been business as usual for many decades, Ecuador, Peru and Bolivia are no longer willing to submit to Washington's free rein in its perceived "backyard". For far too long, the DEA drug control efforts have been completely in non-compliance with international human rights norms and treaties.The DEA's forced chemical eradication efforts have generated some of the most significant collateral damage from the USA's war on drugs without making a significant impact towards reducing the cultivation of coca or poppies (raw material for heroin).

American taxpayers have given the DEA and South American drug enforcement agencies more than 30 years to find an approach that works. They have failed, because it seems that there is no solution to the drug problem as long as demand for cocaine consumption is strong, and illegal profits earned remain staggeringly high.

No country in South America, other than Colombia, is giving away so much of its national pride and sovereignty to US pressure to wage a war on drugs against its own people. Declaring a war on drugs against its own people, the subservient Colombian government is certain to continue producing more recruits for the radical leftist insurgency. The adaptation of the so called "Plan Colombia" is such a case of national submissiveness. It is a creation of the Clinton Administration which implemented it in 1999. Its focal point is to eradicate coca plants by spraying with non-toxic herbicides, to shut down the processing of coca leaves for cocaine production, and to help Colombia fight its more than 40 years of leftist insurgency. During its first 10 years, Plan Colombia has been a US-DEA war on drugs that has been enforced with the support of a small airforce of 86 airplanes, at the cost to American taxpayers of $6 billion dollars. What is unique about Plan Colombia, which is not evident with other coca producing countries, is that the program is well-embedded into the political, economic and cultural *status quo.* The beneficiaries of the status quo are the large military, the various law enforcement agencies, the drug cartels, and the rebel forces (FARC). All have a vested interest in maintaining the present status quo. The military and law enforcement organizations, along with their and their political backers, are lobbying in Washington with everyone they can find to renew federal funding. The drug-cartels are dealing well enough with the illegality of their trade, for the sake of their staggering profits. Lastly, the FARC *guerilleros are* also profiting from the illegal cocaine drug trade by providing protection to drug cartels and coca growers. All share a common denominator– their vested interest in profitability. They are all willing shareholders in the present *status quo.*

Back in 1999, Colombian coca growers alone had nearly 464,000 acres of coca plant cultivation. The failure of massive eradication efforts, is shown by the fact that by 2009, Colombia had more than 576,000 acres of coca cultivation. That is a clear 25% increase. A 2008 UN report shows a 27% increase in coca cultivation over the year 2007. To counter these figures, law enforcement and government bureaucrats have released impressive statistics showing that the Plan Colombia works well, and that they have eradicated hundreds of thousands of coca acres. So far, this is true. But what they are omitting to explain is the 25% increase in coca cultivation. The simple truth is that, as is the case in Peru, Bolivia, Ecuador and the Amazonian region, as eradication spraying takes place in one area, the coca growers simply plan new cultivations in different parts of the country. This has major social consequences. The massive eradication efforts has spawned violence against the rural population who is not part of the drug trafficking culture. As drug traffickers are forced to move their operations to different parts of the country, they push into territories that are not under the "radar" of the eradication authorities. In most cases, peaceful regions are disrupted by violence and death. Drug traffickers and their narco-terrorist supporters become the local authorities who control every aspect of village life. They disrupt the local economy by forcing the change of local crop production from fruits, grains and vegetables to the "cash-production" of coca plants. This also drastically effects the number of livestock, and the overall nutritional intake of the local population. Peasants are forced to comply with the drug culture and are caught between the drug traffickers, the narco-terrorists and the army. For example, in the northern Nariño Province, in February 2008, narco-terrorists massacred 20 indigenous campesinos whom they had accused of being army informers. The massacres of indigenous campesinos is a common event that attracts little or no attention from the national or international media. The narco-terrorists, the army, the rebels, the drug traffickers, the mercenaries and common bandits are all vultures who feed off the miserables. The once peaceful forested areas where peasants live out their productive lives just a few years ago, has now turned into the killings fields of the drug war zone.

When traffickers and narco-terrorists are driven off by fumigation spraying, they leave behind long-lasting human misery. With no government support to re-develop their traditional crop production and livestock, peasant families are splitting-up, with husbands and brothers forced to earn their income by migrating to cities. I have witnessed such mass migrations, while I was residing in Peru and Bolivia. Peruvians migrated from the highlands because they lived in constant fear and suffering due to the destruction of their livelihood. The rebel forces of the Maoist Sandero Luminoso, and Tupac Amaru (MRTA), the security forces, the death squads of the paramilitary, narco-terrorists, the DEA's mercenaries, were all in pursuit of their own objectives. Death and property destruction has caused hundreds of thousands of peasants– mostly non Spanish speaking–to disperse to villages and cities. With no particular modern skills, with limited education and nowhere to house themselves and their families, most have turned to crime. Refugees in their own country, they invaded and occupied other people's properties as squatters. Police and private security personnel were hired to evict them, and this caused additional social problems. As early as 3 a.m., thousands of day workers, street vendors and others would enter the city of Lima to find work, something to sell, or someone to rob, to sell *pasta de coca* (cocaine base) to drug addicts, and to commit other illicit activities. Their children would beg on every street corner, older children would turn into *Piranhas* (street-robbery gangs), their daughters might become prostitutes, and life for most was simply nasty, brutish and short. Again, the magnitude of coca cultivation makes coca eradication in South America an impossibility. It's time to shut down the DEA's eradication program that has failed and has caused so much misery to so many innocent *campesinos*, for such a long time.

Central America, which includes the countries of Panama, Guatemala, El Salvador, Nicaragua, Costa Rica and Belize, is utilized as a mid-point storage and transit region for drugs being smuggled into Mexico. The final destination of drug smuggling is the United States and Canada. Criminal groups in Central American countries are for hire to Mexican drug cartels. They are predominantly smugglers, transporters, wholesalers and distributors of cocaine, marijuana and methamphetamine. These drugs, including Mexican produced heroin, are controlled, distributed and re-transported for the North American drug market. In Mexico, the US drug control policy is also part of the anatomy of failure. Despite recent annual wasteful expenditures of about $20 billion on domestic drug law enforcement and supply reduction, US drug consumption hasn't declined significantly since the Clinton years of the early 1990's. Drug prohibition has failed just as Alcohol Prohibition of the 1920's. The price of Mexican smuggled cocaine, heroin and other drugs has slightly fallen. Even though the severe drug laws of the US has the highest incarceration rate in the world, drug trafficking has not been affected. Not only has the US DEA's anti-drug policy failed to achieve its objectives in Mexico, but the methods used to try to reduce coca and poppy supply–aerial fumigation–endangers and alienates rural communities. Gun trafficking from the US to Mexican drug-cartels is estimated at 2,000 guns per day. This contributes to about 90% of the guns used by Mexican drug cartels against rival drug traffickers and innocent citizens.

As a former smuggler and bootlegger, I can say with conviction and by experience that black market of any sort is encouraged by profits, and absolutely nothing else. So, instead of treating the demand for illicit drugs as a free market, and addicts as patients, the DEA's American anti-drug policies have boosted the profits of druglords the world over. It has fostered powerful drug cartels that would frighten the hell out of Al Capone ten times over. It is simply a delusion to believe in a "drug-free" world, which is no more attainable than a "smoke-free" or "alcohol-free" world. Yet futile temperance and religious rhetoric about winning a war on drugs persists among Washington's warmongers, who are motivated by false morality and ideological bankruptcy. It is always dangerous when ideological rhetoric drives policies that effect the lives of millions of people around the world. Especially so when the war on drugs rhetoric leads politicians, careered bureaucrats and the general public to accept collateral casualties that would never be permissible in non-militaristic law enforcement. Drug prohibitionists still talk about eliminating drugs around the world as though recreational drugs were a plague to humanity. Don't they know that drug control is not like a plague or disease control? Don't they know that that there is no popular demand for smallpox, polio or swine flu? Drugs have been around for many millenniams. Opium and cannabis were grown in ancient societies that still exist today, such as the Middle East, Asia Minor, the Far East and the Mediterranean societies. The same is true for the use of coca leaf in South America in the ancient cultures of the Aztecs, the Moche, the Incas, Ashanicas, Paracas and others. In the last 150 years, synthetic drugs like heroin, cocaine or methamphetamine have been produced in many developed and developing countries. The popularity of certain illegally classified drugs very much depends not just on availability, but also on current fads, fashion trends and cultural traditions. Recreational drugs that are illegal are in competition with alternative legal means of stimulation and distraction.

The delusion that we can reduce the demand for drugs by imposing harsher drug laws matters little in reality, except in militaristic or theocratic states. However logical the desire to reduce the demand for illegal drugs may appear, more punitive drug policies only creates a nation of jailers. But let's be clear, the demand for use of psychoactive drugs is not a new phenomenon, for it is universal and has been part of our human civilization–and mostly not a problem. In fact, I would say that there has never been a drug-free society, regardless of the punitive style of law enforcement. Damage reduction from drug addiction must rely on honest public education, positive alternatives to drug use, avoidance of "zero tolerance" policies, and a 100% legalization of drugs which would be manufactured by legal pharmaceutical enterprises. Driving drug cartels out of business should be the primary goal. The elimination strategy must be simple: reduce drug-use prices, thus making the black market non-profitable. This would have a domino-effect, which would reduce the militarist nature of drug law enforcement, corruption, killings and the suffering of the coca producing peasants. Reducing the harm use of drugs would also reduce deaths, diseases, crime and the suffering associated with drug-abuse and prohibitionist drug policies. So much could be accomplished by legalizing all illegal drugs. It could produce a tax revenue from the legal sale of drugs. It would reduce the prison population from drug convictions. Taxpayers would save money by eliminating the $34,000 yearly prison cost per offender vs. $3,300 for one year of substance abuse treatment. It would reduce street gangs due to lack of drug earnings. It would reduce drug money laundering in Central America. It would help reduce the US budget deficit, and would improve US-Latin America relations. It would eliminate funds for narco-terrorists and political rebels in Colombia, Peru and Bolivia who use their narco-dollars to purchase guns. Furthermore, we have succeeded in relative harm reduction with legal drugs, such as alcohol, cigarettes and coffee, by promoting responsible drinking and designated drivers to avoid drunk-driving deaths. We have persuaded people to cut down on smoking, to seek treatment or to use nicotine chewing gum and patches. We have informed consumers about the effects of coffee and have produced de-caffeinated coffee as an alternative. Legalizing drugs means reducing the transmission of HIV and Hepatitis C through syringe exchange programs and reducing overdose casualties by providing readily available antidotes. In Canada's Vancouver East End the InSight Program allows people addicted to heroin and other illegal opiates to obtain methadone (free of charge) from doctors or pharmaceutical heroin from clinics. Other countries, such as Britain, Germany, the Netherlands and Switzerland, have similar programs. After many years of trial, these drug programs demonstrated a decrease in drug related harm without increasing drug use. Under existing drug law prohibition, however, these programs are not a final solution. They may serve some good, but they are a patchwork and a public relations exercise in civility. Until the legalization of the production and distribution of drugs serves the medical problem of the addicted, we will continue to apply harm reduction measures but not achieve an elimination of harm. Ideological claims of abstinence from drugs or our present exhibition of indifference to the lives of millions of drug addicts, or the well-being of the coca campesinos, is part of the anatomy of our failure.

An area that needs to be looked at closely is the long-lasting mistrust that Latin America has towards the USA. Under the guise of the war on drugs, the DEA has been accused of carrying on policies and militarist actions that are not anti-drug related. In an Agence France-Presse article dated November 6, 2008, the President of Bolivia, Evo Morales, accused the DEA of complicity in the drug trade. Morales stated that throughout the 1990's, the DEA in Bolivia "bribed police officers, violated human rights, covered up murders, destroyed bridges and roads...The worst thing is it [DEA] did not fight drug traffickers. It encouraged it." Referring to the DEA's past actions, Morales stated that after a 1986 operation in Huanchaca National Park, it was determined that the largest cocaine processing plant was under DEA protection. It was also determined that "the DEA has investigated political and union leaders opposed to neoliberal economic policies, which amounted to political persecution." On November 6, 2008, Morales accused the DEA of shooting and killing Bolivians during their anti-drug operations, including members of the coca farmer's movement. It has been confirmed that the DEA, in September, 2008, encouraged political unrest which killed 19 campesinos. Amid fears of possible mercenary assassination attempts, the Bolivian President acquired a new fleet of security vehicles for his personal use and protection. This was a decision made after a plane destined to carry Morales crashed unexpectedly in the Andean region of the country. After much consideration, the Bolivian government ordered all DEA activities suspended and expelled all of its agents, including the US Ambassador Mr. Philip Goldberg. Current relations between Bolivia and the US remain rather distant and continue to deteriorate.

The in-depth revision of current drug policies instituted by the US-DEA on Latin America is even more urgent in light of the enormous human and social cost, and threats to democratically elected governments. The criminalization of politics and the politicization of drug crimes continue to contribute to the corruption of public servants, the judicial bodies, the political system and, especially, to the DEA's law enforcement and to that of their counterpart agencies. Acknowledging the failure of the UN drug policy since 1961, and its consequences, is the inescapable prerequisite to breaking the taboo of opening up the debate for more humane drug policies. We need to acknowledge that the current war on drugs repression policies are rooted in prejudices, irrational fears and misguided ideological delusions. The whole issue of total drug legalization has become a taboo which inhibits rational public debate. It is thus imperative to review critically the deficiencies of the prohibitionist strategy adopted by the ideologically motivated temperance advocates in the United States in the last 150 years. It is also important to question the low priority given to the medical drug problem by both the developed and developing countries in the Americas, and in other parts of the world. We in the developed countries need to change the status of drug addicts from illegal narcotic buyers to that of patients cared for by the public health system. We need to support a public health standpoint for the decriminalization of the possession of drugs for personal use. Finally, each country's progressive people, humanitarian groups and societies, community networks and social commentators must engage the seriousness of the drug problem, and search for policies consistent with each country's history and cultural background. In order to drastically address the drug problem, we must be less focused on repressive measures and more respectful of indigenous people of the world. It is imperative that we debate for effective policies based on scientific knowledge rather than on ideological and temperance/religious biases. The deepening of the debate concerning the current policies on drug use must be rooted in a vigorous evaluation of diverse alternatives to the prohibition strategy. The construction of alternatives must be the product of a plurality of social educators, health professionals, the progressive media, community leaders and the law enforcement institutions. In order to reduce anti-Americanism, we must encourage Latin American social groups to dialogue with American legislators about their civil societies. Only by jointly developing workable cultural and economic alternative to the current war on drugs, can we all reshape the anatomy of failure and engage in more efficient and humane policies. As a former smuggler, contrabandist and bootlegger, my experience has confirmed the causes that terminated my own illegal activities: the total legalization of prohibited products.

10

WAR ON DRUGS: THE HUMAN TRAGEDY

"We don't want the drug fight to be a political tool to defend geopolitical interests. We don't want a drug fight that is a pretext for the U.S. or other powers or governments to simply control [Bolivia's] government, blackmail or place conditions."

Evo Morales - Bolivian President

The organized ideological roots of the current "War on Drugs" began as a religious-moralist popular movement in 1789, led by the American Temperance Society, in Litchfield, Connecticut. Its work in promoting temperance across the USA inspired the establishment of numerous separate and independent Methodist and Catholic organizations. All advocated a form of public morals as was defined by their religious views on human behavior. As a result, strong societal support was encouraged for unified political measures against the recreational use of any sort of intoxicant, including liquor and particular drugs. Both liquors and drugs were deemed to present either unacceptable harm to the community or to impose far too great a burden on the morals of the community. The use of liquor or drugs was regarded as a habit, a vice, and a sign of weakness and amoral upbringing. By 1826, there were 8,000 groups who had started to lecture their fellow citizens against the use of liquor and drugs. By 1839, 18 temperance publications were published with over 1,500.000 paid subscribers.

Things progressed, and by 1880 the Woman's Christian Temperance Union (WCTU) aimed to influence American youth. It established a Department of Scientific Temperance Instruction in Schools and Colleges. Its aim went even beyond educating the youth. The WCTU focused its attention on voters who *"must first be convinced that alcohol and kindred narcotics are by nature outlaws, before they will outlaw them."* It was decided to lobby for legislation to coerce the moral suasion of students, who would be the future generation of voters. Virtually every American state had adopted strong legislation mandating that all students must receive a program of compulsory anti-alcohol/drug education. To be sure, the concrete implementation of the legislation was closely monitored in every school, down to the classroom level, by determined and vigilant WCTU zealots throughout America. There is strong evidence that this compulsory temperance education was a major factor leading to the establishment of

National Prohibition with the passage of the 18th Amendment to the US Constitution.

For decades the battle to establish prohibition was fought in the political arena by conservative and politically right-wing evangelists. They preached the benefits of prohibition and proclaimed that slums would soon be only a memory, that sickness, poverty and crime would be eradicated, telling their parishioners "Let the church bells ring and let there be great rejoicing for the enemy [alcohol/drugs] has been overthrown and victory crowns the forces of righteousness."

The Harrison Narcotic Act was enacted in 1914, prohibiting the freedom to use drugs for any purpose and making free market drugs illegal. It should be noted that before the Harrison Narcotics Act of 1914 there were no federal drug laws in the United States. Moreover, nowhere does the US Constitution authorize the federal government to intrude itself in the personal lifestyle of how one eats, sleeps, drinks or dresses.

By 1918 the Temperance Movement achieved the main goal of passage of the 18th Amendment, establishing National Prohibition. Under this amendment, and the Volstead Act of 1919, which provided for the enforcement of Prohibition, the manufacture, transportation, and the sale of alcohol and drugs were prohibited by federal law. Prohibition effected the quality and price of alcohol, and it also gave rise to violent crime. The undeclared war on alcohol and drug became part of life for the next thirteen years, until 1933. It should be pointed out that the smuggling, distribution and sale of cocaine, heroin and marijuana has been flourishing since the Harrison Narcotics Act of 1914 was implemented. However, the drinking population was far larger than the drug using population. Without abandoning the drug trade, crime gangs saw a huge opportunity to exploit and fulfill a need to provide the public with prohibited alcohol.

And so, the religious delusion of the temperance movement moralists was seen as the magical answer to social ills, where "the *slums will soon been a memory.*" Instead, a militaristic reign of terror began and soon the general public realized that nothing was improved by prohibition. Somehow, social life turned out to be worse than before. Here are some brief statistics for the period 1920-33:

❖ Arrests for prohibition *increased* by 105%.

❖ Arrests for Drunkenness and Disorderly Conduct *increased* by 41%.

❖ Arrests for Drunken Drivers *increased* by 81%.

❖ Thefts, Breaking and Entering *increased* by 9%.

❖ Murder, Bodily Assault and Battery *increased* by 13%.

❖ Federal Convictions *increased* by 561%.

❖ Federal Inmate Population *increased* by 366%.

❖ Total Federal Budget for Prison Institutions *increased* by 1,000%.

As the war on alcohol and drugs became serious, crime became organized. Criminal groups involved in smuggling, producing, transporting and selling booze and drugs organized around the profitable source of income provided by prohibition. The quality of prohibited liquor and drugs declined dangerously concurrent with a manifold increase in price. Criminal groups were *bootlegging*--distilling alcoholic beverages--and in most cases were using *lead coils* and *lead soldering* which gives off *acetate of lead*, a dangerous poison. Many working-class drinkers suffered lead poisoning from alcoholic beverages supplied by unscrupulous bootleggers. Other bootleggers used recipes that included *iodine, creosote,* or even *embalming fluid.*

Political leaders, businessmen, law enforcement officers and those who were able to pay the exorbitant prices for smuggled rum, whiskey or gin were not short of high quality booze. Canadian gin, whiskey and Caribbean rum were easily available to them. The supply of foreign liquor to American consumers was an integral part of the *Rum-Row*--a prohibition era term--referring to smuggling ships loaded with liquor. Ships with smuggled liquor regularly delivered their cargo off the three mile maritime limit of the US coast. There, liquor and drugs were re-loaded onto smaller speedboats to be delivered to their intended destinations. Ports of illegal entry were often in Florida cities, along the cost of New Jersey, San Francisco, Virginia, Galveston and New Orleans. Other notables, as in the case of President Herbert Hoover, often visited the Belgian Embassy to drink alcohol during prohibition, because it was legal, since the embassy was technically not on US soil and prohibition was not in effect there.

MILITARIZATION OF PROHIBITION

Prohibition, called the "noble experiment" by President Hoover, became law in the US on January 16, 1920. Enforcement of the law fell to the Department of the Treasury and the Coast Guard was charged with interdicting the flow of "Demon Rum" before it reached American shores. The first months of Prohibition were deceptively quiet in American cities and entry ports. This no doubt caused further optimism among the prohibitionists of the influential Women's Christian Temperance Society who expected the law to be a magical solution to America's social problems.

Signs of the coming onslaught were not difficult to perceive, however. Seizures of boats smuggling illicit imports and raids on bootlegging warehouses in the cities coincided with the law's inception and received the expected publicity. How serious both enforcement of prohibition and the rise of organized crime would be was not yet clear. In the process of providing the public with prohibited goods, criminal groups resorted to real crimes against other criminal groups, the organized Mafia, the police and any "freelance" street gangs. Lawlessness and murders, robberies and muggings became part of daily life. On the law and order side, the Morrison Narcotics Act of 1914 and the Volstead Act of 1920 formed a common legal opposition against the use and free market of alcohol and recreational drugs. It should be noted that the ideological advocacy of both acts can trace their roots to the first temperance movement in Litchfield, Connecticut in 1789. With the enactment of the Morrison Narcotics Act in 1914, followed by the Volstead Act of 1920, *"Phase One of the Prohibition"* was about to begin.

Armed with the righteousness of their *militaristic mentality*, opportunist politicians, priests and preachers, law enforcement agencies, religious zealots and moralists viewed the *"others"* as less than perfect. Supporters of prohibition nurtured the organizational hostility towards legalization of alcohol and drugs. The Rum War was on. The US Coast Guard maintained military readiness with the aggressive seizure of ships carrying foreign alcohol. An increase in operational budget and personnel is every federal organization's ultimate dream. In pre-prohibition years there were 4000 recruits. The pay was comparable to other military personnel of the era. A new recruit had to make a commitment of four years and drew $21 per month. The lowest ranking officers were paid something less than $120 per month, while the Commander drew $6000 per year. Inshore patrol vessels numbered 26 as of January 1, 1920. Nine of them were turned over to the Prohibition Bureau. In 1921, the first year of Prohibition, the original 4000 recruits now numbered 14,000. A number of Navy destroyers were added to the Coast Guard in order to conduct more than 18,000 routine inspections in 1921 alone. By 1925, a quantum leap in equipment, inshore ships, destroyers and new recruits had become operational, resulting in significantly more warlike tactics in the "Rum Row" confrontations. Agreements among important maritime nations resulted in recognizing the legitimacy of seizures taken from their maritime shores. This added to a more aggressive policy against rum running.

On the opposite side of the law, the most direct effect of prohibition was on the supply and demand for the prohibited goods. Prohibitions raise supply costs because contraband market suppliers face legal punishments for manufacturing, transporting and selling illegal goods. Prohibitions increase demand by increasing the uncertainty about product availability and quality, and increase demand through a "forbidden fruit" effect as well. Consumers crave that which has been forbidden to them. In the thirteen years of Prohibition, enormous fortunes were made by rum-runners, with unconfirmed reports of 700% or more in profits for popular scotches or cognac. If $8 per case was paid the Canadian port of origin, the sale price on Rum Row was $65. Often, the rum-runners boasted of their enormous profits, but they also had to deduct the cost of bribes supposedly needed to stay out of the hands of the US Coast Guard. Diluting the alcohol was standard practice, thus affecting the quality of the liquor. It was cut three times before sale, and cheap rot-gut was commonly palmed off as "good stuff'. Liquor in barrels was mixed with unhealthy industrial alcohol and re-bottled in appropriate bottles with counterfeit labels. Fifty thousand quarts of liquor, pass legally through Nassau and the Bahamas, en route to the US in 1917. By 1922, it had increased to 10,000.000 quarts.

I personally went through prohibition while living in Peru, South America, in the late 1980's and mid 1990's. For political and monetary reasons, the Peruvian Government of President Allan Garcia declared a prohibition on foreign goods and electronic items. It was an attempt to support national businesses and producers against the overwhelming importation of foreign goods. As food shortages began to increase, supermarkets closed down. Large-scale cross-border smuggling of food and other goods became the new reality.

Small and large-scale smugglers smuggled food, electronic devices, etc. They sold their contraband to "wholesalers" who sold to provincial "distributors" who, in turn, sold to "retailers" who sold directly to consumers at exorbitant prices. For example, a small $2.50 jar of peanut butter in a normal Chilean supermarket would carry a "retail" price of $24 in a Peruvian country market. Re-sellers would hoard (hide) food causing additional shortages of essential food supplies. Hidden products would "miraculously" reappear when prices skyrocketed. As a Canadian (gringo) living in Peru, I was discriminated against and subjected to paying double or more the normal exorbitant prices. In order to provide for myself, my wife and my newborn daughter Melissa with the essentials of life, I too entered the contraband trade of smuggled food and industrial products. For the next five years–during prohibition– I became one of the many corrupt people who bribed customs officials, highway patrolmen and truck drivers to deliver my goods to my desired destination. To achieve my aim, I had to falsify documents showing non-prohibited goods, instead of the ones I was actually importing. In time, I became very good at it; other smugglers would contract me to smuggle their own contraband goods. I would keep a portion of my goods for myself and my family. I sold the rest at exorbitant prices. This way, I paid 16 bribes in total for each time I smuggled, plus the costly transport fees charged for illegal goods. I survived the prohibition and also made a lot of money for myself and the rest of my corrupt officials.

When prohibition was lifted, and the national borders were open for the free trade of goods, all the offenders–including myself–went out of business. From then on, importers began to pay their regular sale taxes, import taxes and so on. The prices of goods went back to normal based on the market principle of supply and demand. *A true story !*

Consumers in a prohibited market are increasingly uncertain about product quality. They are right to be. I have witnessed smugglers of bulk butter mixing it with other non-dairy substances in order to increase the "butter" volume and thus increase the profit margin. Since consumers in a prohibited market cannot sue the manufacturers of contaminated goods or complain to proper authorities, there is little or no protection against unhealthy products. This uncertainty equally applies to food, electronic items, heroin, cocaine or any bootlegged items that do not come under the quality control of governmental agencies. I have witnessed commercial containers full of children's toys not suitable for sale because of mistaken design. These were "dumped" for sale in the contraband market. One of those toys was a floating duck like the ones children play with in bathtubs. It was made by a well-known American toy company. When placing this cute duck in the water, it was expected that it would float, as ducks should. Instead, the duckling would side-tip out of balance and float on its side instead of upright. Hundreds of thousands of those defective ducklings were sold on the contraband market of Peru during the early 1990's prohibition. Defective TVs, cameras and electronic items–with well known name brands–were dumped with no consumer protection, and no one of legal authority to enforce quality control.

In the United States, the war on alcohol and drugs was carried out by the newly established Bureau of Prohibition. To deal with the increased crime scene, the US government had to spend millions to finance this department to pay for all its deputies and workers. Typical of prohibition time everywhere, government bureaus were very corrupt. The smugglers, bootleggers and drug dealers made so much money they could afford to corrupt and pay-off members of any department.

The National Commission on Law Observance and Enforcement, Dated January 7, 1931 wrote on CORRUPTION:

As to corruption it is sufficient to refer to the reported decisions of the courts during the past decade in all parts of the country, which reveal a succession of prosecutions for conspiracies, sometimes involving the police, prosecuting and administrative organizations of whole communities; to the flagrant corruption disclosed in connection with diversions of industrial alcohol and unlawful production of beer; to the record of federal prohibition administration as to which cases of corruption have been continuous and corruption has appeared in services which in the past had been above suspicion; to the records of state police organizations; to the revelations as to police corruption in every type of municipality, large and small throughout the decade; to the conditions as to prosecution revealed in surveys of criminal justice in many parts of the land; to the evidence of corruption between corrupt local politics and gangs and the organized unlawful liquor traffic; and of systematic collection of tribute from that traffic for corrupt political purposes. There have been other eras of corruption. Indeed, such eras are likely to follow wars.

For more info: www.druglibrary.org

Operational budgets in government departments dealing with prohibition increased. For example, the personnel of the Custom Service and the Coast Guards increased by 45% and by 188% respectively. The Custom Service budget increased 123% and the budget of the Coast Guard increased over 500%. Both budgets were simply added to the national deficit. It was the most expensive, extensive and sweeping effort to enforce a prohibition law to change the social habits of an entire nation in recorded in history.

The act set January 16, 1920, as the date for Prohibition to begin; the "noble experiment" ended unceremoniously on December 5, 1933. The *First Phase of Prohibition* established by the Volstead Act of 1919 was finally repealed. But the Harrison Narcotics Act of 1914 became the focal point and rallied prohibitionists in their enforcement of the *Second Phase of Prohibition:* the War on Drugs.

THE WAR WITHIN:
1914 TO PRESENT

The US war on drugs can be described in simple terms: The War Within! During prohibitions, the kind of prohibited products or habits are of no consequence, for they can be drugs, alcohol, electronics or style of life. Prohibition is primarily a political decision taken by a governmental authority against what it perceives to be dangerous behavior or dangerous public morals. I think that future social thinkers and supporters of drug legalization will classify the present American anti-drug propaganda on equal terms with the earliest witch hunts and the Crusade wars. I think they will place the American domination of international drug policy, along with the UN Single Convention on Narcotics of 1961, as a hopelessly entangled set of superstitious debates on guiding public morals against the use of recreational drugs. Here, I must re-affirm the fact that I am not launching into an argument in favor of the use of drugs, but rather an argument against the present drug propaganda. The current propaganda is motivated by a philosophical justification in support of militarization against the common person's habits and lifestyle. Iin the final analysis a person's habits or lifestyle is no one else business. In the words of a great American, Mark Twain:

"I have achieved my seventy years in the usual way: by sticking strictly to a scheme of life which would kill anybody else. It sounds like an exaggeration, but that is really the common rule for attaining old age. When we examine the programme of any of these garrulous old people we always find that the habits which have preserved them would have decayed us...I will offer here as a sound maxim...That we can't reach old age by another man's road."

The "war within" includes a war against styles of life that religious moralists with a puritan ideology disapprove of. Their religiosity was quite evident in the temperance movement of the 19th and early 20th. It was not only a motivational force, but a recruiting organizational force to attrack the best people into law enforcement. They were the law and order force against un-American activities, the "force of hope" against the evils of poverty, crime, liberal/free thinking, and the "you are either with us, or you are against us" dividers.

While the temperance movements had lost their public influence by 1933, their relationship to the organizational structure and bureaucracy of governmental departments remained intact. Their philosophy as crime warriors was so ingrained in their institutional structure that it has become inseparable from its present day new objective: the War on Drugs. One must remember that organized crime didn't just disappear after the end of alcohol prohibition. Drug trafficking was still part of the Mafia, street gangs and immigrant-led illegal drug trade. Both illegal drug traffickers, and drug prohibitionist enforcers formed a mutually opposite force. They were, and still are, mutually exclusive, yet interdependent: forces of "good" and "evil", "moral" and "immoral", or "prohibitionists" and "illegal-traffickers." The illegal players were in place, the demand for drug use was apparent, and the forces of law enforcement needed a new purpose for their existence. The drug prohibition of the Morrison Narcotic Act of 1914 would serve them all well. To the illegal drug traffickers, the drug prohibition law served them as a means to gain huge profits and a sense of power. To law enforcement, the drug prohibition meant larger budgets, armaments and equipment, excellent salaries and retirement security, and an "ethical" purpose of life "to serve and secure." Trial lawyers, prosecutors, court clerks, judges, sheriffs, prison guards, prison cooks, drug squads, border-patrols, aerial surveillance pilots, and non-essential personnel were and still are self-satisfied and job-secured. They all look towards the future with self-confidence, knowing that their families and their children's well-being are in good hands. They of the above groups are mutually dependant for their present and future job security.

Right-wing politicians can present their agendas as crime fighters and drug war enforcers. All of it can make one feel cynical. It reminds one of the ancient Greek story of *Atlas,* who carried the Globe's problems on his shoulders. I imagine the miserable, wretched poor junkies in the East End of Vancouver or any other inner-city, carrying the aforementioned comfortable, self-satisfied and "law abiding" citizens on their shoulders. These · pathetic drug addicts, whose medical problems became a criminal offence, are the excuse for someone else's drug war crusade. They all earn their comfortable living on the shoulders of the dreadful drug addicts. Both drug dealers and drug prohibitionists have a mutually undeclared vested interest in maintaining the *status quo. They just happen to be on the opposite side!*

The "war within" on drugs intensified in the late 1930's and early 1940's for two specific reasons. The Mexican-Americans of the Southwestern states were the first reason. It was a well-known fact that the Mexican-Americans were the largest ethnic group who traditionally used marijuana. It was against this ethnic sector of American society that a deliberate harassment campaign was designed to push the Mexican-Americans out of the United States and back to Mexico. Driven by Anglo-American xenophobia and popular racism, this harassment intensified during the Depression era of job scarcity.

The second reason for the intensification of the "war within" on drugs had to do with the powerful influence of corporate America in Washington which led to the prohibition of hemp plant production. Under the guise of temperance, the Du Pont Corporation lobbied for:

"...marijuana prohibition [which] was the covert protectionist activities of the paper and synthetic fiber industries...These interests, of which the Du Pont Corporation was the most important representative, wanted to eliminate possible competition from the hemp plant (marijuana is comprised of the buds or flower of the hemp plant), which had recently

became a serious "threat" as a result of the invention of the hemp decorticator machine. With such a machine in existence, competition could have become severe because hemp, in contrast to trees, is an annual plant with no clear-cutting problem. Hemp also is believed to produce 4.1 times as much paper pulp as trees, acre for acre.

Several trends in government converged to make hemp/marijuana prohibition possible....Andrew Mellon, the chief financier of the Du Ponts, had become Secretary of the Treasury and appointed his nephew, Harry Anslinger, to head the newly created Federal Bureau of Narcotics, and to make its prohibition his agency's top priority. In addition, the recent lifting of alcohol prohibition had confronted a number of federal agents with the risk of unemployment if new forms of prohibition could not be instituted. All these factors contributed to the passage of the Marijuana Tax Act, the initial federal propitiatory legislation, in 1937."

(Associate Professor of Law J. M. Blum, University of Buffalo, May 21, 1990, letter to Judge Elvin, Buffalo, New York).

In fact, there were three reasons for enforcing drug prohibition which had no relation for the so called "dangerous" recreational drug of marijuana. Racism, bigotry and corporate power and influence provided a new purpose for the federal departmental deployment of the war on drugs. More later.

The United States and Canada, are "temperance cultures" to use Harry Levine's words (1992), with a strong popular temperance mentality. This culturally powerful way of thinking was founded and propagated by various pioneer religious sects (Mormons, Methodist etc) in a number of states and provinces. Populism finds its power base in the temperance mentality. It is expressed by defining what is an acceptable behavior and what isn't. It is a consistent and uninformed temperance view on public morals, on abstinence from drugs, alcohol or pre-marital sex, as being the only acceptable lifestyle. Society's problems are easily attributed to whatever temperance leaders deem serious enough to consider their attention: Sunday shopping, gay-marriage, children's education, lack of praying in schools, end of life rights etc. In short, temperance mentality is both moralistic and accusatory in their claims of the causes of social ills. Any deviation from temperance remedies is now most often associated with the social ills of sexual promiscuity, family break up, domestic violence, AIDS, child abuse, atheism, socialism and addictions of all sorts, as all being harbingers of the imminent end of the world itself. Temperance thinking advocates prohibition, abstinence or reduction harm of social problems. Whatever its vitiation, it still leaves the temperance mentality largely intact. Solutions can be achieved through Biblical Commands, or obedience to certain temperance remedies and definitions for or against "good" or "bad". For obvious reasons, not all temperance claims are false; some alcohol and drug problem do exist. What is the object of dissent, however, is the temperance doctrine that does not allow other people to practice and choose what works for them.

By the 1950's, the temperance mentality had enormous institutional influence and support among legislators, including those who funded drug law enforcement, drug research, and drug literature conforming to their own assumptions. Yet, they suffered ideological setbacks in the public's "heart and minds." Their arguments were incoherent and unfounded and were ignored by the public. Since the premises of the temperance movement grew from a religiosity of moral ideology rather than from fact and scientific evidence, their arguments were discredited empirically. What the champions of temperance had, however, were the politically led opportunists who held positions in governmental agencies fighting on a "new" war-front: the war on drugs. Their popular support, however, was based on the demoralised ignorance of the religious fundamentalists. To give much needed concrete legal and political legitimacy to their existing institutional support, prohibitionists found an international forum: the United Nations.

The 1960 UN Single Convention on Drug Control, with its subsequent re-affirmation in 1971 and 1988, has seen nations around the world implement a legally binding drug control system. As of January 2005, the Single Convention had 180 signatory nations. The SCDC is a monolithic doctrine that places existing international drug control treaties into one instrument that supersedes any nation's new treaty. For example, recently the Russian Minister of the Interior, Mr Boris Gryzlov, confirmed before the *State Duma* that *"total prohibition of illicit drug use was not the government's own initiative...but rather the result of our responsibility to implement the UN drug control of 1961, 1971, and 1988."* An important force in sustaining this Convention is the United States of America. As its staunch defender, it is the US that maintains and enforces the Convention's disciplinary framework.

Internally, political, ideological and economic policies have long-supplanted the 19th century's puritanical and religiously moralistic notion of prohibition. Through the strategy of moralistic issue linkage, the fundamentalists of the religious right have certainly exploited their hegemonic socio-political status for the defence not only of American drug prohibition, but of UN global drug prohibition as well. This all powerful UN-USA doctrine has produced a formidable alliance. It has made it difficult for any nation to deviate significantly, or even to contemplate deviation, from the monolithic doctrine of prohibition. Trade consequences are tied to UN certification as an important means of enforcing its war on drugs. The annual certification process on a nation's efforts to suppress drug use and trafficking has been fortified by the US's efforts to conflate its war on drugs with the cross-border fight against organized crime. Such a strategic move has increased the implication of any nation's deviation. Any attempt to reduce the drug war effort is potentially damaging for a nation's international image. Clearly, maintaining the doctrine of the global drug prohibition at the UN level is important because it helps Washington to legitimize both its domestic drug policies and the militarization of its many overseas activities involved in its war on drugs.

Domestically, based on the latest newscasts, most law abiding Americans may think that the war on drugs targets shady characters in dark alleys, drug smugglers, motorcycle gangs, organized crime, and Mexican-American or African-American "king-pins." Middle-class parents, in particular, do not imagine that their "little-Johnny" or their "little-Jane" can be arrested for criminal drug offences. After all, these kids may be attending the local high school or college and be involved in sports or yoga classes. Could these kids be "A" students as well?

Yet, *Crime in America FBI Uniform Crime Report 2008* statistics show that a total of 1,702,537 people were arrested for drug violations. Of those, 847,863 were arrested for marijuana related offences. Of those, 754,224 were arrested for marijuana possession alone and 93,640 persons were arrested for marijuana trafficking. This equation leads to 852,864 people arrested for victimless offences involving marijuana. It should also be noted that there are between 140 and 190 million Americans (2007) who smoke marijuana. What is disturbing, however, is that all of the 754,224 arrested solely for possession of marijuana will be stigmatized with a criminal record for the rest of their lives. A criminal record usually interferes with employment and sensitive goverment positions etc. Could one or more of those be your "little-Johnny" or "little-Jane"? Most parents know that adolescence is a period in which a young person rejects conventionality and traditional parental authority in an effort to establish independence. For most adolescents, the exhibition of personal independence may consist of engaging in a number of risky behaviors including the use of a forbidden fruit like sex, drugs, alcohol, or staying out late at night, in order to fulfill a daring challenge or to find one's self. Most youth overcome this tendency and assert their independence in a constructive rather than in a destructive manner. Most parents recognize that such adolescent behavior is an essential part of growing up. One does not have to be a PhD to know this, for after all, all parents were adolescents once upon a time. Why then do we pass laws prohibiting and criminalizing such adolescent behavior, if it doesn't harm another person? Why do we treat the realism of what it is to be young as our domestic enemy, and conduct the war on drugs against our youth? Is it possible that this realism, may even include medical benefits? Researchers at the University of British Columbia, Canada, concluded:

"Thematic analysis revealed that these teens differentiated themselves from recreational users and positioned their use of marijuana for relief by emphasizing their inability to find other ways to deal with their health problems... These teens used marijuana to gain relief from difficult feelings including depression, anxiety and stress, sleep difficulties, problems with concentration and physical pain."

(www.drugwarfacts.org/adolecents)

The US, whose federal and state legislation serves as a model for international drug control agreement and who claims leadership in the global anti-drug fight, the War on Drugs, has seen a rapid and dramatic increase in the prison population that started in the mid-1960's. By the mid-1980's, 34% of federal inmates were incarcerated for drug violations; by 1995 it had increased to 60%, and by 2000, 91.4% of all federal incarcerations were for drug possession and trafficking. The average time served in prison is 55 to 76.6 months. Jail time served for drug offences are second only to that for violent felonies. According to the American Corrections Association (2006) the average cost per day per inmate in state prisons alone is $67.55, which calculates to more than $17 billion per year. Between Federal and State prisons, the cost of maintaining drug offenders is more than 30 billion per year.

Could we instead invest this amount of money to fight the War on Poverty in Inner Cities? Why do we have such lopsided priorities? *God protect our children from drug prohibition!* I said children, because the average state offenders is under 18 years of age. One statistic shows that between 1980 and 1997 the under-age arrests of drug offender went from 2% to 11% of all drug offences.

For more than 95 years (1914), the US prohibition policy has resulted in the following socio-political and human drama:

❖ Prohibited drugs are even more widely available, in an ever- widening circle of crime.

❖ Prohibition has created the illegal drug trade and the groups who profit from it.

❖ The criminal drug trade is multinational, called Cartels, Mafia, Cosa Nostra, Triads, Families, Narco-terrorists, motorcycle gangs etc. They threaten personal peace, and security and political stability throughout the world. Militarist actions by law enforcement agencies make people's safety much worse or more fragile.

❖ The failure of drug prohibition has transformed the issues of personal choice and personal health into a worldwide criminality. This criminality stigmatizes young people and also endangers their lives and their health and safety by forcing them to consume contaminated diluted illicit drugs.

❖ Those tempted by drug addiction are thrust into contact with diseases, the worst being AIDS, HIV, Hepatitis 2.

❖ Regular drug users are driven to crime and prostitution to finance their drug addiction.

❖ Governmental drug distribution of prescribed drugs to drug addicts costs far less than the cost of keeping them in jail.

❖ 65% of women in federal prisons and 29.1% of women in state prison have been incarcerated for violation of drug laws.

❖ Good intentions must not be translated into bad laws and a threat to civil liberties. The enforcement of the bad laws of prohibition has won no advantages for individuals or society.

CALLING THE "DOGS OF WAR"

In the name of the War on Drugs, much of Colombia, Peru, Mexico, Ecuador and Bolivia have being subjected to terror, massacres, assassinations, rapes, kidnappings, bombings and the environmental destruction of their jungles. The rebel armies of the Colombian Revolutionary Army Forces (FARC) in the South, the Army of National Liberation (ELM) in the north of Colombia, paramilitary right-wing groups, narco-traffickers, DEA agents, Israeli, Australian, British and American mercenaries are all fighting for or against control of narco-dollars and the coca and poppy fields. Mercenary special forces train the private armies of drug traffickers to protect their coca and poppy fields against other drug traffickers and the DEA's chemical spraying. After more than 50 years of trying to stop the flow of Colombian cocaine and heroin into the US and Europe, the violence caused by these conflicting groups resembles the Vietnam conflict. Although the paramilitary and mercenary groups are private and illegal, they still receive aid and political support from Colombia's police and army. Because the US aid to Colombia includes armaments, it is indirectly supplying the paramilitary and mercenary groups. Because of the intensity of drug-related violence, more than 2 million people became internal refugees when they lost their small farms due to the US program of fumigating coca lands. US military power and influence in the Americas is being used to support the white minority of European descent to subdue the indigenous population. This was a colonial policy practiced by Spanish and Portuguese *conquistadores* of the 16th century. I have witnessed myself the effects of post-colonialism that continue today against indigenous peoples who work in mines and on plantations. This small, white ruling class controls Latin America's political life and most of its wealth. As a result of the previous importation of African slaves, Colombia now has the third largest black population in the Americas, after the US and Brazil.

Because of its proximity to the USA, Mexico has long served as the mid-point or stopover for Colombian's drug trafficking. The militarization of the War on Drugs in Mexico is taking place among rival drug cartels, government police and military forces, and the DEA's agents. Mexican drug cartels have existed and operated for many decades. Most began as marijuana growers and traffickers and evolved into middlemen between Colombian's drug cartels and the US drug consumers. As the Mexican drug organizations began to cultivate their own coca and opium crops, they began producing their own cocaine and "brown-heroin." With the demise of Colombian's Cali and Medellin cartels–after Pablo Escobar's death in the 1990's–the Mexican cartels began to share in the wholesale illicit drug market in US and Europe. There are eight major cartels in Mexico who control most of the drug trafficking: the Sinaola, the Juarez, the Tijuana, the Matamoros/Tamaulipas, Los Negros, Los Zetas, La Familia Michoacana and the Beltran Leyva cartel. The country's violence has grown due to such endemic social factors as the severe, often brutal war on drugs. Mexico's land itself is rich in natural resources and the economy is somewhat productive, but the political disempowerment of more than 90% of its citizens is problematic. This is a potential threat to the relatively small white ruling class who control Mexico's land and political power. To protect both, the Mexicans are staunch supporters of US military spending on the war on drugs. Against this force, are the rebel *Zapatistas*–through their political actions against the mercenary narco-terrorists. Paramilitary mercenaries are financed and used by large landowners to defend their property against rebel peasant incursions. Narco-terrorists who operate independently are also hired and used by druglords to protect their illegal trade. Mexican-American teen gangs from across the border are recruited as hired killers for competing drugs cartels. The end result of all these conflicting forces is the perpetual suffering of the campesinos and their community leaders. Such conflicts are conducted and financed by narco-dollars and the US's funding against drug trafficking.

The Peruvian National Police (PNP) is a militarized police force. Peru simply lacks a civilian federal police force. Thus, the war on drug operations are conducted primarily by the PNP. Although the Maoist rebels were largely eliminated by 1993, a surviving faction of the Shining Path–*Sendero Luminoso*–guerrillas continue to launch counter-offensives against the anti-drug police unit of the PNP. The war on drugs is therefore conducted between the PNP, the rebel forces and the narco-traffickers in one of Peru's main coca-growing and cocaine producing regions of the Apurimac, the Ene river lands and the Huallaga valley. A number of narco-terrorist groups are in alliance with the Shining Path and the drug cartels. Their support base is the tens of thousands of *campesinos*–peasant farmers–who grow coca leaves on an estimated total of nearly 18,000 hectares in these regions alone. Due to a lack of transportation routes for their perishable products, the peasants have no choice but to cultivate coca leaves. This product helps them to increase their meagre income by growing coca and producing coca base–*past de coca*–the intermediary product used to manufacture cocaine. If the drug business is eliminated, the local economy will suffer, especially the coca growers. There is strong evidence that the rebels are involved in the production of cocaine which finances their armed conflict. Their aim has always been to consolidate their support base among the coca growers, and to secure the flow of chemical input and cocaine output in the manufacturing process.

Economics therefore motivates the co-operation between the rebels/narco-terrorists, the coca growers and the narco-traffickers. When the illegal drug trade is reduced or eliminated, the rebels/narco-traffickers suffer from it the most. Financial help for the indigenous farmers to grow alternative products will increase their living standard through fair-trade policies. Usage of coca leaves is not restricted to cocaine production. As the Bolivian President Evo Morales declared: *"la coca no es cocaina"* [the coca leaf is not cocaine]. The Bolivian government insists the coca leaves can be converted to tea or other medical products. On a number of occasions, while visiting the jungles of Bolivia, I drank coca tea with or without meals. I can testify that at no time did I ever get "high" from drinking coca tea. During my years in the towns, villages, cities and the jungles of Peru, I have had coca tea, especially when travelling the high altitutes of the Andean Sierras.

The US's war on drugs is not a just war. It is an all inclusive militarized policy for eradicating the coca plant with the aim of eradicating drug trafficking. Planting coca leaves is not the same as manufacturing cocaine. The coca plant is an agricultural product that has digestive and curative qualities with proven health-related usages. It also provides the hundreds of thousands of campesinos with a honest but low standard of living. It is because of these considerations that the Bolivian government decided in November 2008 to opt out of the US war on drugs. The Bolivian President Evo Morales, an indigenous coca farmer himself, suspended the militaristic activities of the US Drug Enforcement Administration in Bolivia. Morales defended his decision by declaring that *"There have been DEA agents who, carrying out [illegal activities], financed rogue groups [mercenaries]...."* I have, in fact, seen and known mercenaries who carried on with their search and destroy missions in both the Bolivian and Peruvian jungles. I didn't have to know the details of their actions, but as the old saying goes, "if it looks like duck, quacks like duck, walks like duck, then it must be a duck." The DEA's war on drugs conducted through "rogue groups" is a well-known open secret. It has caused the deaths and poisoning of hundreds of indigenous people. The direct search and destroy missions on the ground and the air campaign to fumigate/eradicate the cultivation of coca leaves has disrupted the livelihood of thousands of Bolivian peasants. Politics, economics and cultural misconceptions on both sides have resulted in an unjust war, with the Bolivian people as its main victims.

11

STRONG ARM ECONOMIC

...FAIR TRADE OF COCA LEAF PRODUCTS

"The prestige of government has undoubtedly been lowered considerably by the [drug or alcohol] law. For nothing is more destructive of respect for the government and the law of the land than passing laws which cannot be enforced."

Albert Einstein

"Fair Trade" is a humanist concept that has been around since the early 1980's, starting in Germany. But the formal classification scheme didn't get off the ground until the late 1980's. *The World Fair Trade Organization* (WFTO) outlines several essential principles of fair trade. These basic principles convey that, regardless of where we live, we share a common goal: to earn a honest living, to provide for our children, and to have gainful employment that brings dignity and a sense of accomplishment. Fair trade therefore refers to helping producers to build a sustainable future, and consumers to develop a humanist conscience about the origin of their products. Both consumers and producers need to respect and support each other so that fair earnings can be made through the paying of fair value for products.

Coca leaves are mistakenly related to the singular product of cocaine. Yet, coca leaves have many other mineral and alkaloids that are useful for the commercial production of medicine, food, and cosmetics. The time has come to correct the ideological temperance error responsible for including coca leaves along with the hazardous classified substance of cocaine. Such an error, and its subsequent policies against the production and consumption of coca products, has caused severe economic difficulties for the indigenous population of the Andean/Amazon region. Millions of campesinos in Peru, Bolivia, Colombia, Venezuela and Ecuador have been subjected to inhumane abuses based on other people's ideological interpretation of coca leaves. *Coca Leaf is Not Cocaine !* Humanists around the world who dare to recognize this dreadful mistake need to repeal the UN Conventions that include the coca in its drug control measures. Would the UN ever consider outlawing the cultivation of grapes because one can extract alcohol from it that can cause alcoholism? Of course not, because *Grapes Do Not Cause Alcoholism!* Humanist and Fair Trade organizations would be *on par* with governments of several South American countries, such as Peru, Bolivia and Venezuela, who are defending and championing the traditional and modern uses of coca leaves and its extracts. Pan-economic (not ideological) measures need to be applied, because the lack of economic considerations causes ethical and trade unrest. Having said that, there are coca extracts in toothpaste, teas, chocolates, soaps and shampoos, granola bars, cookies, hard candies and herbal liqueurs, including de-cocainized coca extracts. The popular energy drink *Red Bull Cola* contains natural flavouring from de-cocainized coca and Kola-nut extracts. Each can of Red Bull Cola contains 0.13 micrograms of cocaine. This 0.13 micrograms of cocaine does not cause any harm to consumers. This has been confirmed by Bernhard Hoffman, a food scientist for the *Nort Rhine-Westphalia*. This Austrian food scientist states that a person needs to consume 120,000 litres of Red Bull Cola before he/she is harmed. However, many countries around the world have banned this popular drink out of irrational fear and ignorance of the scientific evidence. Other popular drinks in Germany, such as Pepsi One and Diet Coke contain 0.13 micrograms of cocaine flavouring. This does not mean that the above companies are adding minute amounts of cocaine. Rather, this 0.13 micrograms is what still remains when 99.87% of the cocaine alkaloid is removed through the de-cocainizing process. Again, in all of these popular drinks, de-cocainized coca leaves are used for flavouring purposes. As of 2008, Red Bull Cola has been sold in Austria, Canada, Czech Republic, Belgium, Britain, Egypt, Germany, Hungary, Ireland, India, Italy, Romania, Russia, Poland, Switzerland, Thailand, the United States, Peru, Bolivia, Venezuela and other countries. In 2007 and 2008, I visited old friends in Peru. I was there for more than nine months, and I consumed traditional coca-tea many occasions. Upon returning to Canada, I noticed that I still had a box of coca tea bags which I had bought in the supermarket. These coca tea bags are sold in all the up scale and open markets of Peru. I offered coca-tea to visiting friends who reluctantly accepted. You see, they feared that drinking coca tea would get them "high." Their reluctance was genuine, but it was still based on ignorance caused by propaganda about the coca leaf. Fear and misinformation about coca leaf products has led people and political leaders around the world to unjustified conclusions.

Beyond South America, most countries' laws (and people's attitudes) do not distinguish between coca leaf and other by-products containing cocaine alkaloids. Thus, the simple possession of coca leaves–as in coca tea–is illegal (except for de-cocainized processed coca leaves). This means that coca leaves are legally listed under opium laws, and in the same category as cocaine. Yet, according to the Bolivian press, the Coca Cola Co. legally, but secretively, imported 204 tons of coca leaves in 1996. The Stepan Company, Natural Products of Maywood, New Jersey, imported 174,000 lbs of coca leaves in 2009. This company has the major monopoly for supplying de-cocainized coca to Pepsi Cola and Coca Cola for use in energy drinks. My point is that there are confirmed usages for coca leaf in the popular drinks of *Pepsi One, Red Bull, Coca Cola and Dellisse*, which is commercially sold as coca-tea. There are also unconfirmed reports that the popular energy drink *Gatorade* uses de-cocainized coca extracts for its flavouring. When one looks at the vitamin and mineral content of coca leaves, its inclusion in the energy drinks is justified. Analysis conducted by Peru's state-owned National Coca Co. *Empressa National de la Coca* (ENACO) shows that each 100 grams of coca leaves contains the following:

Nitrogen	20.06 mg	Alkaloids (non-volatile)	0.70 mg
Fat	3.68 mg	Carbohydrates	47.50 mg
Beta carotene	9.40 mg	Alpha carotene	2.76 mg
Vitamin C	6.47 mg	Vitamin E	40.17 mg
Vitamin B.1	0.73 mg	Vitamin B.2	0.88 mg
Niacin	8.37 mg	Calcium	997.62 mg
Aluminium	17.39 mg	Barlum	6.18 mg
Iron	136.64 mg	Strontium	12.02 mg
Boron	6.75 mg	Copper	1.22 mg

Zinc	2.21 mg	Manganese	9.15 mg
Chromium	0.12 mg		

Mixed with other herbs and natural stimulants, the coca leaf is an integral part of commercially produced energy drinks for athletes and active individuals. One must also recognize the nutritional value of the coca leaf and its traditional use, on the basis that *"the coca leaf is not, in and of itself, a narcotic drug or psychotropic substance."* The fact is that the drinking of coca-tea in South America, or of fortified de-cocainized energy drinks in North America and Europe, is carried out daily by millions of people. Some of the indigenous people's use of coca tea dates back over the centuries.

I believe that the argument as to whether to legalize coca leaf outside of the South American region is a *Catch-22* legalistic entanglement. It is grounded in an irrational set of conclusions that were rooted in the report written by a group of UN unqualified investigators led by a banker named Howard Fonda, who briefly visited Peru and Bolivia in 1949. The *Commission of Enquiry on the Coca Leaf* report was published in 1950. It concluded that the effects of using coca leaf–chewing it or brewing it as a tea–were negative, even though the report defined the chewing of coca as a custom rather than as an addiction. From the 1980's to the present, a number of scientific investigations have concluded that the 1949 report was arbitrary, not scientific, racist, bigoted and overly-broad. A number of legal attempts have been made by Peru, Bolivia and Venezuela to untangle the legalisms of the UN, in order to recognize the traditional use of coca leaf. So far, all attempts have not succeeded, because the UN is still bound by its original pre-conceived project to "investigate the effects of chewing coca leaf and the possibilities of eliminating production and distribution." Yet, the production and distribution of coca leaves is legally well established in South America, and the de-cocainized coca extracts are well-used by the giant conglomerate makers of energy drinks. The difference between the legal and illegal definition of coca leaves is the measurement of 0.13 micrograms of ineffective cocaine found in Red Bull Cola. Remember, it takes the consumption of 120,000 litres of Red Bull Cola for someone to get high or hooked from the de-cocainized coca extract. Natural Peruvian and Bolivian coca leaf contains 0.9% cocaine, while the Colombian coca leaf contain 0.1%. This is because some coca species have higher cocaine alkaloids when grown in the high altitudes of Peru and the Bolivian Andean region. Is the marketing difference between natural and de-cocainized coca products as clear as coffee and de-caffeinated coffee? Or, are the differences purely legalistic. Are the Red Bull Cola, Pepsi Cola and Coca-Cola corporations using the legal definition of "de-cocainized" coca extract as a legal means of by-passing the UN's and the USA's prohibition of distribution and sale of coca leaves?

The following may be of interest to legal minds:

US Department of Justice   Drug Enforcement Admin.

Office of Diversion Control
Notice of Registration - 2004

FR Doc 04-5476
[Federal Register: March 11, 2004 (Volume 69, Number 48]
[Notices]
[Page 1 1663]
From the Federal Register Online via GPO Access [wais.access.gpo.gov]

DEPARTMENT OF JUSTICE

Drug Enforcement Administration

Import of Controlled Substances; Notice of Registration

By Notice dated November 4, 2003 and published in the Federal Registrar on December 2, 2003, (68 FR 67480, Stepan Company, Natural Products Dept. 100 W. Hunter Avenue, Maywood, New Jersey made application by renewal to the Drug Enforcement Administration (DEA) to be registered as an importer of Coca Leaves (9040), a basic class of controlled substance listed in Schedule II.

The firm plans to import the coca leaves to manufacture bulk controlled substances.

No comments or objections have been received. DEA has considered the factors in Title 21, United States Code, Section 823 (a) and determined that the registration of Stepan Company to import the listed controlled substances is consistent with the public interest and with United States obligations under international treaties, conventions, or protocols in effect on May 1, 1971, at this time. DEA has investigated Stepan Company on a regular basis to ensure that the company's continued registration is consistent with the public interest. This investigation included inspection and testing of the company's physical security systems, verification of the company's compliance with state and local laws, and a review of the company's background and history.

Therefore, pursuant to Section 1008(a) of the Controlled Substances Import and Export Act and in accordance with Title 21, Code Federal Regulations Sec. 1301.34, the above firm is granted registration as an imported of the basic class of controlled substance listed above.

Dated, March 3, 2004

William J. Walker,
Deputy Assistant Administrator, Office of Division Control, Drug Administration.
(FR Doc. 04-5476 Filed 3-10-04; 8:45 am)

BILLING CODE 4410-090M

How it came about for this corporation to 'unofficially' de-criminalize coca leaves is of no consequence. What is most notable, however, is the fact that under a purely marketing scheme, coca leaves become another trading product. This is the "strong arm" of economics, where in a potential market, there is a potential profit to be made for producers, processors and distributors. Therefore, de-cocainized coca leaves can be marketed as original coca-tea, coca with mint, coca with camomile or sweet grass etc. As for de-cocainized coca extracts, these can be used as stimulants for energy drinks, coca-gum, flavouring for baking, beer and wine making (Coca wine) and other consumer products. Diet control lab experiments conducted in Trujillo, Peru, indicated that feeding animals 150 micrograms daily of de-cocainized leaves significantly reduced their weight. My point is that using a pan-economic approach to distributing natural or de-cocainized coca leaves or extracts for consumer products would set the stage for the gradual deterioration of the present state of legal monolithic prohibition. There is no need to legally challenge the monolithic power of the UN Convention of 1961 in the Hague world court. It would be fruitless and time-consuming. Instead, it is the widespread commercial introduction of de-cocainized coca-leaves and extracts into the capitalist market that will tear down the walls of prohibition.

Furthermore, one must remember that as of 1906, cocaine was illegal and could no longer be used as an ingredient in Coca-Cola's syrup mixture. Yet, the author Mark Pendergrast in his 1993 book *For God, Country and Coca Cola,* reveals a 1933 handwritten formula that still contained coca and Kola-nut extracts, both of which are stimulant drugs. The author came across the following recipe among the papers of Coca-Cola's inventor, John Pemberton.

Flavoring

* Citrate Caffeine, 1 oz.
Ext. Vanilla, 1 oz.
Flavoring, 2.5 oz.
** F.E. Coco, 4 oz.
Lime Juice, 1 Qt.
Sugar, 30 lbs
Water, 2.5 Gal.
Caramel sufficient

Oil Grange, 80
Oil Lemon, 120
Oil Nutmeg, 40
Oil Cinnamon, 40
Oil Coriander, 40
Oil Neroli, 40
Alcohol, 1 Qt.
[let stand 24 hours]

Mix Caffeine and Lime Juice in 1 Qt. Boiling water and add vanilla flavoring when cool.

* **Citrate Caffeine** stands for Kola nut.
** **F.E. Coco** stands for coca leaf extract.

It should be pointed out that the recipe's coca leaf extract was not de-cocainized. The coca leaves still contained a natural 0.5% alkaloid cocaine content. If this recipe was still in use 27 years after cocaine became illegal, no evidence exists showing cocaine-addiction caused by drinking Coca-Cola. I believe that the de-cocainized process is just a legal superficiality over the legal definition of the cocaine content coca leaves. The Coca Cola formula is one of the most closely guarded corporate secrets in America. Could this secrecy be a publicity stunt just like Kentucky Fried Chicken's secret eleven herb and spices recipe? Coca Cola concedes it uses a de-cocainized flavor essence of the coca leaves, one of the few stimulant ingredients the company will publicly acknowledge. It maintains that the coca leaves are one of the ingredients that add to the flavor profile of its popular drinks. It appears that the Coca Cola company is caught in a Catch-22 legal entanglement. If it removed the coca leaves from its product manufacturing process, it could no longer legally defend its trade mark of "Coca" Cola. Thus, an elaborate extraction process to de-cocainize the coca leaf was devised in order to by-pass the legal obstacle of the coca's illegality. In fairness to the Coca Cola company, it insists on a high quality of de-cocainizing from the Stepan company. The Stepan company's elaborate extraction process is highly hygienic. It begins by grounding coca leaves, mixing them with sawdust, soaking them in bicarbonate of soda, boiling them with toluene, steam blasting, mixing with powdered Kola-nut, and then pasteurizing the whole mix. This ensures the DEA's conditions and that it will pass the spot inspections successfully. It is from this sense of fear of the DEA that both the Coca-Cola and the Stepan company are sticklers on security and quality.

The prohibition of newly introduced products in the western world is well documented. Coffee and tobacco were initially amongst those prohibited products. In the 17th century, the Imperial Russian Czar Michael Federovitch executed anyone who dared to use tobacco, and the vassal Prince of Waldeck enforced a hefty fine on anyone who dared to drink coffee. The chronology of the prohibitions on coffee, tobacco, alcohol and psychotropic stimulants is long. Most of the products were driven out of prohibition by the forces of economics and by popular demand for their use. Most of the prohibited psychotropic stimulants are presently classified as prescription drugs under a legal definition which makes their marketing possible. Alcoholic beverages such as wine, whiskey, rum, ouzo, grapa and rice wine are an historical inheritance passed from one generation to the next, forming part of the origins of a nation's cultural identity. Whiskey can be identified by its connection with the Scottish tradition, wine with the French or Italian tradition, ouzo with the Greek and rice wine with the Japanese. These products are promoted in tourism and by commercial enterprises. They are supported by their local and national governments and are seen as being vital to their economies. None of these products are identified with alcoholism, although alcoholism is a potential but not an eventual factor. Prescription drugs also have a *potential* factor of addiction but not an *eventual* addiction. If the latter were true, then anyone one who is using prescription drugs is also a drug addict. Drug, alcohol and tobacco abuses, therefore, are not ingrained in the product itself, for abuses and addiction are human factors. This means that the green coca plant is not synonymous with the addictive white powder of cocaine. It is simply not a synonymous factor.

In the long list of prohibitions, no other natural product has been more criminally subjected to suppression than the sacred coca plant. This plant is native to the South American biospheric environment. It grows in the epicentre of a vast pharmacopoeia of medicinal plants, in the largest and most biologically diverse tropical environment on earth. The Andean-Amazonian region supplies the world with preventative cures from plants like Coca leaves, Una de Gato– Cat's Claw– *Uncaria Fomentosa,* Anahuasca (*Baninsteriopsis caapi),* and Chucruna *(Psychotria viridis).* Without the anaesthetic properties of the coca leaf the Incas could not have performed brain surgeries. Without the curative properties of the Una de Gato, the Ashanicas Indians of Peru could not have cured many tropical diseases and infections. My emphasis is that the coca plant should be viewed for what it is : a medically curative plant, a source of food extracts, a source of minerals and vitamines, a source of cosmetic ingredients and parts of the cultural identity of an ancient peoples.

We in the New World have all come from diversified ethnic backgrounds. In our striving to shape our "New World" we've become alienated from any sense of ancient cultural traditions. We are obsessed with the "new" and "sameness" for all. Industrialism and consumerism have moulded us into believing in a corporate culture of consumption. We have become more legalistic than humanistic, and more obstructionist against those "others" who do not fit in with our own delusions. The indigenous people of the Andean-Amazonian region have been chewing, brewing, cooking and baking with coca leaves for thousands of years. The absurdity of the UN Annual Report of 2007 is evident, as it urges the governments of Colombia, Peru, and Bolivia to take measures to prohibit the sale, use and exportation of coca leaves for purposes which do not follow the monolithic UN drug control treaties. Furthermore, the UN/USA's drug policy attempts to force these governments into establishing as a criminal offence the brewing of coca leaves to make *mate de coca,* flour, chewing gum, hard candies or other products. This will devastate the economic efforts of these three governments in their quest to develop and expand markets for coca products. In response to the UN's obstructionism, the Bolivian government of Evo Morales, a *cocalero* leader himself, declared in defiance, *"In Bolivia, there will never be a policy of zero coca. To do so, would walk over the rights of millions of Bolivians for whom coca is a symbol of our cultural identity."* Millions of South Americans vigorously oppose the UN/USA's war on drugs that include the eradication of the popular coca plant. One bloody lesson the US can learn from the Vietnam war is that there is no military or legal power on earth that can go against a populist movement.

One of the most powerful weapons the South American governments have against the USA's policies on coca leaves is *public relations.* Public relations (PR) is the specific practice of directing communication between an organization–*Empessa National de la Coca*–and the public– American, Canadian or European. PR therefore has the aim of involving the public in a non-tangible way. The fundamental technique used in PR is to identify the target area. In the coca leaf PR, the target areas are the socially conscious youth, the supporters of the Amazonian ecosystem, organic food supporters, naturalists, holistic practitioners, natural mineral and vitamin promoters, environmentalists, amateur athletes and consumers of energy drinks etc. Here are some useful ideas for the South American states:

❖ Create a group of national youth volunteers for the promotion of indigenous culture and coca products.

❖ Train Cusco tourist guides to connect the history of the ancient city with the ritual indigenous use of coca.

❖ Hire Internet-savvy individuals to create strategic powerful press releases for the American/Europeans.

❖ Create press kits and online media kits (foreign).

❖ Use inexpensive blogs to generate traffic, and publicity (foreign).

❖ Create TV public relations with community oriented public broadcasting in English and Spanish.

❖ Create special events, radio & TV talk shows using articulate English speaking indigenous men and women.

❖ Create Internet/Web PR information using Twitter.

❖ Create media kits on the medical benefits of coca leaves.

❖ Create easy to read informative booklets in English, French or German and give them to tourists, free of charge along with urging them to write to Parliamentary leaders in support of indigenous people and of legalising coca products.

❖ Show business opportunities dealing in coca goods.

❖ Develop close relationships with numerous Fair Trade organizations from around the world to trade in coca products as energy supplements.

❖ Concentrate public discussions on Coca-Cola's and Red Bull's use of de-cocainized coca extracts only to have fairly traded coca products used in energy supplements.

❖ Create a Nutritional Symposium that can bring together medical experts, nutritionists, CEO's of food processing companies, local businesses and officials related to exporting and investment.

❖ Peruvian and Bolivian Embassies and Consulates must employ qualified PR personnel to visit food processing and related food companies and invite them into participate in Nutritional Symposiums.

The emphasis should be placed on grassroots strong arm economics that can develop a successful marketing effort. Educating tourists and academics who visit Peru and Bolivia can serve to create a credible, voluntary PR force that would carry the coca leaf message forward. Using their influence upon returning home, they can become the coca's voluntary cheerleaders and help the grassroots momentum.

The present state of affairs between Bolivia, Venezuela and the United States is based on a continuation of a historical confrontational attitude by both sides. The nationalist pride of standing-up to the hegemony of the USA is a fine psychological boost for local politics. However, the necessity of eliminating the perpetual poverty of the coca *campesinos* is a practical problem that needs a practical solution. Peru is a fine example of putting life's practicalities ahead of ideological pride. During the late 1980' and early 1990's, prohibition was the result of the leftist policies of President Alan Garcia. My smuggling and bootlegging activities were the result of the opportunity provided by prohibition. Political activists and nationalists were content, as were the offenders who took advantage of the opportunity presented. "God" and "Country" were on the side of those who "stood-up" to the USA-IMF's policies. Ideological confrontation may have been the natural outcome of the long rooted mitrust between both sides. But the Peruvian people could not subsist on ideology and nationalist pride alone; political speaches and rallies are one thing, governing is another. This concept seems to have been rooted in the new political reality of the same President Alan Garcia, who took exception to new economics set by the ex-President Alberto Fumitory. While revisiting Peru in 2007 and 2008, I noticed the great economic advantages the people of Peru had achieved, all but the coca campesinos who were still living in extreme poverty. Millions of campesinos suffer because they are caught between the US puritan monolithic ideology and the national pride of Venezuela, Bolivia and Peru. Colombian strict anti-drug policies which appease the US, and the political military threat of FARC leaves little room for improving the lives of the coca campesinos. The inclusion of the coca plant in the 1961 UN Single Convention is clearly enshrined in the traditional USA's puritanical view, which equates coca with cocaine, and regards both in exactly the same way. The classification of the coca plant as a drug is clearly at odds with the UN's Declaration of Indigenous Rights approved in 2007, which upholds and protects cultural identity and practices such as the chewing of coca leaves.

Prohibitions against public customs and habits have never been successful. Prohibitions may work within a small religious group, where obedience to the ideology is absolutely monolithic. However, the over 50 years of coca prohibition, imposed upon millions of people, indigenous or not has never been successful. It is against this background that we must understand the importance of the grassroots PR that is aimed at condemning the erroneous fact that most of the coca leaf production goes to illegal laboratories for cocaine production. This is our chance to put the record straight. Coca products are increasingly being used in different parts of the world. The socio-cultural stage has being already been set up by social groups, such as the urban middle class in Europe and the US, who receive and use coca. Today, all open-minded progressive people are witnessing the revival of the nutritious coca leaf and the real economic opportunity for the creation of an international coca market. This is not surprisingly, since the coca extracts are used in energy drinks and are considered a mild stimulant comparable to caffeine. Not only that, it has also been scientifically proven that the sacred coca leaf, in its natural state, does not affect public health or the social order. Taking it off the UN's and the US's list of narcotics would normalize the relationship between the US and the coca producing nations. It would restore the latter's national pride; it would protect the cultural integrity of millions of indigenous people and help them out of poverty. Above all, they would no longer have to live in the shadows of coca leaf prohibition.

12

ECONOMICS AGAINST DRUG TRAFFICKING

"When society turns the sick into criminals
then we're all repeat offenders"

Unknown

Declaring war on drugs has become a defining feature of US foreign relations in most of Latin America. Countries like Peru and Bolivia have been encouraged to adopt strict anti-drug law enforcement to combat the illegal production and exportation of cocaine. The degree of anti-drug enforcement is tied to US assistance in the form of foreign aid and loans through the International Monetary Fund (IMF). Trade concessions are shaped to US policy objectives. Economics and anti-drug law enforcement efforts are tied to US prohibitionist policies which are significantly financial in nature. In both Peru and Bolivia, the drug export industry is a leading market force and an integral component of the formal and informal economy. Since legal and illegal markets are often inextricably intertwined, the "narco-dollars" stimulate the very illegal drug market which the US is attempting to prohibit. In short, Peru and Bolivia don't have a significant drug problem. It is the US who has the significant drug problem because of its large appetite for the consumption of illegal drugs—so much so that US drug consumers spend 40 billion dollars a year on recreational drugs. The revenues generated by the "narco-dollars" of the illegal drug industry, however, is not regulated by the national economy. This fact reduces the ability of the Peruvian and Bolivian states to create distinctions between legal and illegal markets.

The enormous global market demand for illegal drugs is an economic force. Although illegal, the global drug market can be seen as part of the broader international economy. Market-oriented opportunities facilitate the illegal drug trafficking. Cocaine serves as the leading generator of foreign exchange, national and international money-laundering, and provides the drug traffickers with the greatest returns in the global economy. In this context, the Peruvian and Bolivian national economies and their banking system cannot carry out the necessary economic reforms needed to finance their heavy foreign debts. Due to the IMF's harsh demands for heavy payments of debts, they have had to prioritise their financial obligations in their internal economic environment. US foreign aid and trade favours are conditioned on Peru and Bolivia's compliance to the IMF's economic guidelines, and on the intensity of their war on drugs. Peru's failure to comply with these guidelines in the 1990's came at a high cost. The IMF's credit was restricted, which left Peru with few options but to refuse to allocate more than 10% of its export earnings to serve the foreign debt.

The measurements used to track compliance with US drug control demands showed the Peruvian failure in the amount of drug seized, coca crops eradicated and traffickers arrested. This led to further economic sanctions and a cessation of American foreign aid. The left-leaning government of Alan Garcia quit the war on drugs campaign putting the economic progress of his country ar risk. In the broader economic context, the national remedy of these economic ills was the nationalization of American dollars–a major currency security against inflation–in both individual and business accounts. This followed a number of import trade restrictions, prohibitions and sky-high custom taxes, which accelerated the Peruvian economic crisis. In a relatively short time, prohibition restricted raw and processed food and equipment supplies, medicine, transportation and luxury goods. The economic turmoil caused by prohibition began in 1985 and lasted until 1995.

Prohibition has been practiced throughout human history. It was used as a restrictive instrument of moral and ethical behaviour in the form of religious taboos against promiscuous sexual acts, homosexuality, or in marriage to delineate the roles of men and women etc. It has also been practiced against the consumption of certain foods (Muslims and Jews do not eat pork), alcoholic drinks or recreational drugs. Prohibition can also be used as a political, ideological and economic instrument. Under the political system of communism, owning private property was prohibited. In the Peruvian case, the economic restrictions of prohibition were the result of legal constitutional decisions as was the US Drug Prohibition Act of 1914 or the Alcohol Prohibition of 1920. Therefore, prohibition is a multifaceted repressive legal tool available to the political system of the day. In the market place, prohibition is directed against specific products, making the production, distribution and sale of those products illegal. A natural result of such market conditions is the appearance of an illegal market. Such illegal markets still function on the general economic fundamentals of supply, demand and margin of profitability. How does this illegal market function? What are its main characteristics? I believe that I know the answers to these questions because I was not only a witness to prohibition but also an active smuggler, bootlegger, distributor and seller of contraband goods.

The only reason that I and other contrabandists entered the illegal trade of goods is money. And a lot of it!! All other non-material reasons are, in fact, secondary in importance. There is no romantic element to this kind of illegal activity. No daring Hollywood heroes exist in any illegal market scene. Excitement is only caused or created because one is not careful enough to avoid law enforcement traps and informers. One's day begins the same way that it finishes—looking for buyers who are able and willing to buy one's goods. As in both legal and illegal markets, the supplier seeks to market the kind of goods that will maximize his/her profit margin. In my case, I would smuggle unadulterated well-known brands of whisky for consumers who were willing to pay the extra cost to indulge. Most of my consumers were looking for other liquor-brands. All of them, however, bought what I was offering them. I was the one who controlled the market, not my customers. I have known other bootleggers who maximized their profits by adulterating their already cheap brands of whisky, rum or vodka. There was no legal regulatory authority to prevent them from doing so. Their end-product contained no regulated measurements and the alcohol adulterants were of unknown quality and origins.

Because of the uncertainty of supply, people's demand for goods was far greater than the products that were available in the market place. Looking at such a situation one could see that the legally imported items were far less expensive than the contraband products. Lack of foreign currency, however, restricted everyone's contraband business. That is, until each contrabandist was able to accumulate more wealth and invest a lot more in the smuggling business. Taking chances, buying cheap and selling expensive, and being more creative in smuggling routes all could contribute to the quick rise or fall of any risk-taking illegal entrepreneur. From strictly a business point of view, I could not see any recognizable differences between legal and illegal market principles. The bottom line was the guiding god of one's daily business affairs. From the law enforcement side, criminality, corruption, deceit, threats, fear, "close-calls" to one's personal safety, ruthless competitors, greed, and widespread thievery were simply the norm rather than the exception. The contraband market could not help the government out of its budgetary difficulties. Marketing logistics of the economic benefits of legalising, regulating and taxing the underground market were even more compelling particularly as the government's budgets were stretched so thin that they could no longer afford to maintain basic social securities, hospitals, schools, police and army etc. I could not help but notice that consumers would much rather purchase legal products with an added excise tax on them than continue to purchase products illegally. The underground market had inflated prices due to costs related to its illegality. Economic arguments have fallen flat with prohibitionists thus far, not just because of ideological reasons but also due to their vested interests. Loss of tax revenues combined with the ever increasing cost of law enforcement, arrests, trials and imprisonment produce a further budgetary cost to state and federal governments.

I have to admit that my own vested interests were with the prohibitionists. They were my "bread and butter" supporters. Without prohibition, I would have long gone out of business. After all, I was there for the money, not for any ideological glory. Profiteering therefore is the only motive for contrabandists to enter the illegal trade of goods. This style of illegality is a characteristic of prohibition whether it is in the US against drugs, in Peru against certain imported goods, or in Saudi Arabia against liquor importation and consumption. In other words, the absurdity of prohibition is not an exclusive characteristic of the US temperance movement. This is because prohibition is a worldwide ideologically motivated imposition on people. In the US the ideological roots of prohibition originated with the puritans and religious moralists of the 18th and 19th centuries. In Peru, prohibition was imposed by left-wing ideologues as a political stand against the US and the IMF's hegemony. Today's alcohol prohibition in Saudi Arabia is imposed by the religion of the Wahhabi theological fundamentalists whose delusions are imposed on people's daily life. Prohibition therefore is a social-conservative ideology operating under any language, ethnicity, country or political system. It is not based on a rational system of thought. The US militarization of the "war on drugs" is an irrational "overkill" approach over the medical problem of the few and over the recreational habits of the many.

For more than five years, I was an active smuggler of goods and bootlegger of Canadian and Scottish whiskey between Peru and Chile. During that time, I came to a basic conclusion: how can a government be so stupid as to permit illegal traders to exploit and profit from people's personal vanities? Recreational drugs have been used by North and South American indigenous people, in the Caribbean religious ceremonial tribes, by the ancient Greek future-tellers, by the Hebrew and Egyptian civilizations, and by our contemporary pleasure seeking youth. Having "fun" has always been against the core of Christianity's dogma. Obedience and personal suffering brings you closer to God than having a drink, using drugs, dancing, engaging in pre-marital sex, or seeking an alternative spiritual fulfillment. It is the religiosity of the temperance power structure that still controls the US ideological crusade against drug use. It is the moralists' battle cry of today, as it was during the McCarthyism of the 1950's and later in Reagan's crusades against "un-American" labour unionists and their popular activists. No single federal political leader in the US would put his/her future on the line to campaign for the legalization of all drugs. But there are a number of backroom political bureaucrats who are working towards the de-criminalization of drug possession. I'll come back to this point.

During my contraband years, my 'work' took me to many large and small cities, states and provinces throughout the eastern part of South America. Police and paramilitary law enforcement units were on constant alert for vehicles and trucks carrying hidden contraband products. Highway and open market sellers and people whose houses serviced the contraband trade were constantly on the look-out for the state units whose task included the confiscation of any contraband. The financial burden to pay for law enforcement units placed the state apparatus in financial ruins. State budgetary overruns for law enforcement, judicial overload and the imprisonment of contrabandists was more than the local governments could handle. The phenomenon of de-criminalization of possession, distribution and selling of contraband appeared in the poorest towns and villages. State and municipal budgetary difficulties forced local administrators to look for rational ways of solving their financial burden. They found it! Necessity is the mother of invention. A non-legalistic rule became the rational solution to the tax evasion and free market principles of the smugglers. By decree, any contraband within the town's limits were permitted to be sold openly. Contraband merchants needed to be registered with the local municipal authorities in order to be protected from confiscation of their goods. How those goods got into the towns was of no concern to the local authorities. A reasonable fee was collected from each merchant, and a daily rent fee was collected for the space occupied in the local open markets. One could see the town's rent collector (escorted by police) issuing each merchant a receipt for the paid fee. At first, most contrabandists were reluctant to display their goods openly. Secrecy had become a habit! In time, other municipal leaders would visit the now "free markets" to discover means of generating with much needed income. You see, it was the basic income vs. expenditures economics that forced rational thoughts into their minds. Had these local authorities waited for a solution from the central federal government prohibition would still be intact. By taking a locally initiated income-tax "harm reduction" approach to their financial problems local governments undermined prohibition at the same time. In the last two years of prohibition more and more cities and towns throughout Peru were trading freely and collecting fees.

The "reality check" came with the federal election of President Alberto Fujimory. Negotiating with the IMF and US policy makers was not an easy political act. The reality of free market economics brought about the proper administrative border apparatus, a newly established Customs Service, Income Tax Service, import permits, sale permits and related general revenue. At the end of two years, those economic policies ended prohibition, and drove me and hundreds of other contrabandists out of business. It was as simple as that! *It's the strong arm of economics, stupid!* In short, prohibition can be destroyed from within, state by state, city by city, until the federal bureaucrats can no longer afford to fight against their own kind. Free market oriented President Fujimory realized this while he was campaigning. The administrative apparatus of prohibition was chipped away slowly but surely.

The same economic phenomenon of chipping away that drug prohibition in California appears to be taking place slowly but surely. While the federal laws are against the selling of drugs, the economic realities that state and municipal authorities face will eventually destroy the American drug prohibition. Licence fee, business taxes, income and salary taxes etc., will provide local governments with an incentive to legalize recreational drugs.

The Peruvian lessons to be learned are priceless. By the end of 1996, criminality and corruption related to smuggling and bootlegging ended unceremoniously. Offenders who were arrested while committing robberies or kidnappings against smugglers and bootleggers still had to serve their sentences. Most of the smugglers who were accustomed to the trade became law-abiding businessmen who now paid their taxes, invested their money in their own businesses and hired people to work for them as import-brokers or tax-accountants. Also, once those who were involved in the illegal contraband and bootlegging trade had a legal method of settling business disputes, the number of attacks on competitors dropped significantly.

In the US today we also see a similar movement chipping away at the monolithic block of drug prohibition. Grassroot organizations are actively promoting the de-criminalization of marijuana for personal use. This is only the beginning. Many states, including the State of California, Oregon and others, are on the road towards legalizing the use of marijuana. This means that for the first time, laws are being passed legalising the use of a drug. What moved politicians to legalize the use of marijuana is partly due to economics. The financial burden of law enforcement's war on drugs and the overcrowded judicial and prison system for drug-related offences has uprooted the budgetary balance. As the general economy faces further difficulties, politicians have had reason to look for ways of raising capital to meet their overbearing budgetary needs. Look at Los Angeles, California. More than 1,000 shops are selling medicinal marijuana; legislators are looking for a means of taxation. Billions can be collected to pay for social services, public health, education and social "cushion" programs. The side effects of the US economic crisis of 2009, its double-digit unemployment and massive housing foreclosures, has forced state bureaucrats to look at legalization of soft drugs as a rational means of taxation. As with the reality check in the Peruvian provinces and towns, the strong arm of economics is playing a key role at chipping away at the monolithic block of prohibition. State legislators from around the US are viewing California's legalization of marijuana use. Its free market approach has not created massive "Reefer Madness" on its users. The question is, as the novelty of the forbidden fruit runs its course with teenagers, will there be a decline in the use of marijuana? We all have to wait and see !

Let us now look at the problem of drug prohibition in the US and around the world. There three issues: a) the role of narco-dollars in the economies of drug producing countries b) organized drug trafficking and c) the prohibition's war on drugs.

It is viewed that the role of narco-dollars in the drug producing countries of Peru, Bolivia, Colombia, Mexico, Afghanistan etc. is an economic issue and that it shapes the relationship between the national governments and their private sector markets. There is no clear-cut distinction between state and private market relations. Both legal foreign exchange and illegal narco-dollars are intertwined and integrated into the national economy. For example, during the 1970's and 1980's the construction industry in Miami, Florida, was booming. Commercial real-estate space, expansion of port facilities, shopping malls and related tourism development were far ahead of any other sector in Miami's economy. Much later, it was discovered that narco-dollars from drug trafficking were invested in the local economy It was the extensive development of these economic sectors that brought about the law enforcement's attention. These kinds of local financial investments also helped reduce the trafficker's risk of physically transporting their narco-dollars back to their own countries. *(I had the same problem in Peru during prohibition. In fact, I had to cut-off the hydro power to most of my house plug-ins and stuff them with contraband-dollars. Police searches never suspected my secret stash, hidden behind the jack-covers).* Some of these narco-dollars are invested back home to maintain the traffickers' lavish lifestyle and to contribute to low level public works in their own towns. These financial contributions are also an integral component of the private sector markets. Indeed, the revenues and employment generated by these investments have actually helped keep the local economies more secure from financial difficulties. But the most important and the largest recipients of narco-dollars are the guerrilla anti-government forces. These forces provide security and operating licences to both the peasant producers of coca leaves, cocaine producers and large-scale drug traffickers. Hundreds of millions of narco-dollars are freely exchanged among drug traffickers, corrupt politicians, police, paramilitary forces, legitimate business enterprises, bankers and financiers, the coca growers and the leadership of the twenty thousand strong guerrilla armed forces of Colombia. This has been an important basis for financing the last 40 years of Colombia's internal warfare. In Peru, the once thirty thousand strong *Sendero Luminoso* guerrilla force extorted hundreds of millions of narco-dollars to finance their 20 years of warfare against the government. This money was used to purchase guns, ammo, food, supplies and to pay for their own corrupt politicians who supplied them with intelligence. Afghanistan's opium narco-dollars have financed the Muslim Taliban and Al Queda terrorists. In Mexico, drug trafficking gangs are the major intermediaries transporting cocaine and/or producing heroin and marijuana for the USA drug market. These are the major players whose vital interests lie with the continuation of US and UN world drug prohibition. They're all benefiting from the *status quo*: local governments and their national economies, their law enforcement, the cocaine producers, the coca plant peasants, the large drug traffickers, corrupt politicians, the rebel army and others. After all, what do you think would happen to their main source of revenue if today's illegal drug trade becomes legal tomorrow and cheaper to produce? Can the strong-arm of legalization and free market economics be used against them! *"Its plain economics, stupid! "*

Organized drug trafficking is not simply about conducting victimless business. Starting at the coca plant level, most coca leaf producers are making a meagre income. Isolated in the jungles of Bolivia and in the coca triangle of Ecuador, Peru and Columbia, these producers and their families are living below the poverty line. Most coca leaves are sold to processors of *pasta de coca* who are also mostly hidden in the jungles. Processing coca leaves into coca-paste is not done in a hygienic working environment. The chemical fumes, lack of clean water, the constant threat of being discovered, robbed, killed or kidnapped, are facts of life. After much work and financing their own purchasing of chemicals, their profit margin is also meagre. At $800 US per kilo of gross profit, they are lucky if they net more than $100 US. They are forced into perpetual poverty, with no medical care, suffering from chemical side effects, generally living alone and away from their families. All this so they can provide the world's pleasure seekers with the luxury of recreational drugs. There is no Fair Trade marketing for their products. They cannot demand to be paid more. They're not organized or regulated, nor are they educated in marketing, nor are they supported by their own governments, nor are they enticed to adopt better quality control, as are the coffee growers of Brazil, Costa Rica, Colombia etc. I have seen their deformed bodies, their pathetic existence in perpetual misery. The same applies to the small-scale cocaine dealers who work for the drug cartels. I have never seen a wealthy small-scale drug dealer living in a comfortable home. Most are living in the poor *barrios* and *pueblo jovene* in the shanty towns of Brazil and Colombia, the *Canto Grande* of Peru etc. The average US and Peruvian street dealer is a working poor who holds a low-wage job and peddles drugs part-time to obtain drugs for his own use. Earnings from illegal trading are a supplement to legitimate employment earnings. I am certain that the coca growers and producers will be the only ones who will benefit from the legalization of cocaine. Legalization of cocaine will mean a well regulated agricultural sector of the national economy, producing a hygienic drug under strict guidelines. They can be organized into Fair Trade agricultural bodies who can be scientifically educated on drug toxicity and content measurements. Under such drug legalization, the cartels will no longer be in control; the killing, torturing and corruption will stop, as will the present worldwide human misery. Cartels will no longer be able to force the coca growers to live a "nasty, brutish and short" life. Instead, the strong arm of rational marketing economics will drive the cartels out of business. *"Its plain economics, stupid !"*

The present US prohibition's war on drugs has resulted in many prosecutions that are instituted without sufficient evidence to justify them. In many drug cases, unwarranted drug squad searches and seizures are made, which results in a number of false arrests or court dismissals of the drug charges. In other cases, the honesty and credibility of the DEA's drug agents are in question. At times, the agents court testimonies and theatrics have successfully distracted jurors and judges from paying attention to the actual evidence. This is not done randomly. The prohibition law enforcement agencies are more concerned with "head-count" than with upholding the spirit and letter of the law. They are more concerned with publicized mass arrests of small-time drug dealers than in bringing to court carefully prepared cases of some importance. The mass media publicity created by these large-scale arrests ensures the maintenance of their organization's budgets. The bottom line of the game are the "head-count" statistics, written, reported and presented to the Ministry of Justice. This is not unique to the Drug Squad law enforcement alone for it is in the nature of every organization to keep increasing its size in order to survive and perpetuate itself. Most organizations are social, economic or technical/service, and thus victimless. What is unique, however, is that prohibition's militarized-arm also perpetuates the human misery it causes by the mass arrests done to increase the "head count". This enlargement of bureaucratic power, at the expense of civil rights, always results in the abuses of power which inevitably occur. The magnitude of the drug enforcement task is far greater the law enforcement can handle effectively. Uncertainty exists as to whether drug enforcement can subdue national drug trafficking. Small-scale drug dealers deal in relatively small drug volumes, and are comparatively easier for drug enforcement to handle. It is also evident that prohibition law enforcement's violation of civil rights is the task of arresting large-scale traffickers. For the last four decades the work of prohibition has proven increasingly more inadequate. This has created a strong and growing public opinion on the futility of the law enforcement of prohibition. In its attempt to aggressively enforce national drug prohibition, enforcement has been taken to another level. On the assumption that it is of national interest, prohibition enforcement overlooks constitutional guarantees and legal limitations. In this sense, drug law agencies yield to the convenience of enforcing prohibition as they see fit. Simultaneously, drug trial lawyers, prosecutors and the courts have created an "assembly-line" justice system where a plea-bargain "pull-chain" keeps rolling to clear pending drug cases at maximum bureaucratic speed and convenience. Lawyers convince their clients to plea-bargain to lesser charges "or else the prosecutors will ask for the maximum sentence." This threat scares the "pants-off" the street drug dealers who, like most of us, know little of the law. The prosecutors, using their own legal jargon, may or may not follow through with asking for a lesser sentence. The judges are neither here or there in regards to the evidence; they follow procedural court rules, rather than listening to time-consuming justice pleas. At the end of the day, these run of the mill procedures are classified as "a job well done." But the hundreds of thousands of sentenced inner-city minority dealers, teenage "pot-heads", skid row revolving-door offenders, free-thinking spiritualists, medical drug addicts and weekend pleasure seekers are all unwilling assembly line clients of a long lost justice system. Ironically, one may accuse me of being a lawyer basher. But I am less disdainful of assembly-line justice than William Shakespeare, who in 1604 said, *"The First Thing We Do, Let's Kill All the Lawyers."*

The obvious solution to reducing the economic burden caused by the war on drugs and by prohibition's assembly-line justice system is to legalize drug possession. Clearly, when prohibition ended in Peru, I was driven out of business. There is no mystery to it! In the case of drug legalization in the US and around the world, it would be the economic death to the drug cartels from Colombia to Mexico, including the US organized drug gangs. The economic crisis of 2009 has truly eliminated the money to continue the war on drugs. Once again, as with the Alcohol Prohibition of 1920-33, we can no longer ignore the well-documented collateral damage of the Drug Prohibition of 1914. The only "benefit" derived from the war on drugs is that it keeps the prison, justice and law enforcement industries filled with hundreds of thousands of employed guards, police, prosecutors, public defenders and probation officers. Ending drug prohibition is not a "silver-bullet" solution to our drug problem. But it would save us from something far worse, the human tragedy caused by the assembly-line justice system and the revolving door of the prison industry. It would put drug addiction in the hands of the medical profession, where it was before 1914, until we decided to call the drug squads on our children.

The good news is that the monolithic block of drug prohibition is beginning to be chipped away at slowly and effectively. Working around the United Nations and US legal definitions of drug prohibition, a number of countries have partially de-criminalized the possession of drugs for personal use. Non-enforcement for both possession and production of marijuana for personal use is in effect in the Netherlands. Public opinion for non-enforcement is widely supportive and has also influenced the courts which have repeatedly ruled against the government's prosecution based on individual cases. Netherlands' public opinion is an integral part of a cultural attitude of *gedoogbeleid* - tolerance- which regards soft drugs such as marijuana as being not important enough to spend limited resources on. Drug addiction is seen primarily as a public health issue. It is because of this health issue that public drug responsibility is mainly shaped by the Ministry of Health and Sports, with the assistance of the Ministry of Justice.

As is the case with many countries, full jails, stretched state and local budgets and general weariness with the prolonged war on drugs have made prohibition harder to enforce. On the federal level, President Obama's administration has announced that registered marijuana dispensaries will no longer be raided by federal drug squads. In Vancouver, British Columbia, Canada, "shooting galleries" and decriminalization of personal drug possession suddenly looking more permissive. Argentina, Brazil, Peru, Mexico, Spain, Portugal, England, Denmark, Germany, Latvia, Slovakia and Croatia have all decriminalized the possession of small amounts of drugs for personal use. In California, the system of medical use of marijuana that people have adopted is in fact a version of legal legislation. Elsewhere in the US, there other signs of chipping away at the monolithic block of prohibition. Some 14 states have versions of decriminalizing the personal use of soft drugs for medical reasons. Other states have adopted a $100 civil penalty for possession of marijuana. California and Massachusetts are holding legislative hearings on bills to legalize marijuana outright. In Europe, authorities face similar pressures connected with budgets of enforcement, bursting court-schedules and prisons. Experiments like these seem to have been noted in the White House. President Barak Obama, when asked about legalising pot, said that the issue is a "non-starter." Yet, Obama has called the war on drugs an "utter failure." It remains to be seen whether these efforts at chipping away at the monolithic block of prohibition will help stem the bloodshed that has engulfed the drug wars in the Americas. The bullet-weary citizens of the Americas, the people of Afghanistan and those in the line of fire of Mexico's trafficking wars are living in some of the riskiest places on earth.

Here, we must tackle other issues. Personal possession and decriminalization, though helpful as harm reductionist in many ways, won't do much against organized crime, nor towards establishing Fair Trade with the coca growers of the Americas and a free market within a well controlled business environment. On key element need to be discussed: prevention vs. crime-reduction.

PREVENTION

Prevention concentrates on the *root source* of a given social problem and induces practical steps for eliminating its causes. What is the *root source* of drug trafficking? Marketing illegal drugs. I believe that behind every great fortune (legal or illegal) there is a crime, whether it is drug trafficking, defaulting on mortgages, tax evasion or borderline illegal offences, predatory lending etc. From the cocaine producers in the jungles of Peru, Ecuador and Colombia, to the small or medium-scale drug dealers, up to the drug cartels and international drug trafficking groups all are there to make money. *The source-root is drugs*; the *end-gain is money*. I have already stated that I went into the smuggling business for the money. The *root source* were bootlegging and imported goods. The *end-gain* was my unlawful accumulation of money. In the medical area, the *root source* of obesity are trans-fats and lack of exercise (among other reasons). In this case, eliminating the consumption of trans-fats and engaging a moderate exercise program would have the *end-gain* of eliminating obesity. The elimination of my bootlegging was accomplished by the re-instatement of free market principles as related to alcohol and foreign goods. This terminated the *root source* of my bootlegging and ended the continuation of my illegal business. From this, the *end-gain* resulted in people's freedom to purchase legally produced liquors at regular liquor-stores, to pay regular prices and taxes, and to be assured that their goods were regulated by the government. The re-instatement of regulated open market principles eliminated the *root source* of my illegally accumulated *end-gain*. I can testify that this alone eliminated the *root source* (illegal contraband*)* of the *end-gain* of my illegal profits from contraband.

CRIME REDUCTION

Crime reduction enforcement is punitive as related to drug trafficking. The full force of the punitive arm of law enforcement is applied as a means of fighting and controlling crime. Fighting crime at the street level, or directed against white financial fraud or against organized crime groups is its focal point. Methods used against particular criminal activities vary in the degree of actual public harm caused. Fighting crime is the rally cry of law enforcement units. Part of the crime fighting against the production of cocaine is the chemical eradication of coca cultivation. This is a controversial strategy that is aimed at the eradication of coca plants whose leaves are used for the production of cocaine. This punitive strategy is being pursued as a crime control method against the cocaine drug. Many poor *campesinos* have turned to the cultivation of coca because in many remote areas the transportation infrastructure for perishable fruits is not available. Coca leaves are easily transported and have a long-lasting storage capacity. The coca eradication consequences are felt by the *campesinos* who depend on coca cultivation for their earnings. They bear the burden of the efforts to control the illicit drug trade. As fast as coca-leaf production is eradicated in some areas, the cartels of Colombia, Peru, Bolivia and Argentina open up new cultivation areas. This repetitive struggle between law enforcement and the cartel crime organizations has been going on for over forty years. No clear-cut successes or failures are notable against the eradication of coca. More airplanes are used to chemically spread the eradication of coca leaves. More and more, the consequences of chemical environmental pollution are noticeable in the health of the rural population of *campesinos*. Next in line is the law enforcement against the chemical companies who sell the products needed for the manufacturing of cocaine. Large quantities of chemicals are imported and clandestinely transported into countries that produce cocaine. There is no accounting of the quantities of chemicals that are imported for use in cocaine manufacturing. As some shipments of these chemicals are confiscated, many others pass through port and highway patrols. Corruption in the form of bribes to police and custom officials is the main stumbling block to controlling chemical importation and transportation. As crime fighting is a means and an end unto itself, so are criminal activities.*(During my smuggling days in Peru, I was visited by a person who had a tanker-truck of sulphuric acid for sale. This is a main chemical component in the production of cocaine. This tanker-truck with its sulphuric acid was hidden in a terrorist area, which explained the extremely low price of the chemical. I was told that the original destination of the sulphuric acid was a car-battery plant. This was a lie. I simply refused the offer, not wanting to be any part of the drug trade. There were other more "noble" ways of making money)*. In short, crime fighting against the unauthorized sale of chemicals for drug manufacturing is a never-ending story of an unsuccessful struggle.

Crime fighting against the illegal transportation and distribution of drugs from the producing to the consuming countries is designed to disrupt this prolonged criminal activity. Since the establishment of the war on drugs in 1961, the US and European countries have spent hundred of billions of dollars for logistically and tactically combating the on-going smuggling of cocaine, heroin, marijuana, and so on. Despite the logistical power of the law enforcement agencies for surveillance guidance, high-speed ships, coastal patrol boats, air space radar detection and border-crossing searches, these crime fighting tools are at best hit-and-miss preventative measures. The clandestine transportation of drugs is renewed, expanded and organized into disciplined major criminal conglomerations. These are usually headed by Colombian and Mexican kingpins in the Americas. On the law enforcement side, there has been some major interruption in drug smuggling. But the extensive drug smuggling is always a step ahead of the drug law enforcement. Ports between Haiti and Mexico, Jamaica and the Caribbean island nations are used as a stop- over to the next destination.

Crime fighting as related to the drug trade is structured with each departmental section concentrating on their own area of responsibility. Beyond their specified area of responsibility, each body has a collective "non-investigative" attitude that does not question its own existence. The organizational aim of its members is geared "to do their best" under the circumstances. Specification of aim and separation from non-organizational issues serve as a moral relief for their collective psyche. Benefits or social harm questions are not included in their organizational operating philosophy. Their social isolation is not recognized by them, because it is disguised by their over-inflated organizational self-esteem. Any questions leading to the total legalization of drugs would mean the eventual reduction of their organization's size and logistical power structure. This is not because their members have no cares beyond their narrow goals - it is because any alternative legal options will drastically affect their own self-interests, comfortable earnings and personal purpose in life. The *root source* of crime fighting is crime itself–as a means and end unto itself. The *end-gain* is the direct economic benefits to the organizational structure and its members.

Legalising recreational drugs, including the highly addictive ones, can be done by the strong arm of economics. It would terminate both the *root source* and *end-gain* of drug trafficking and the economic conglomerate of organized crime. By this, I do not mean to open the floodgates of drug availability to the public, as is presently done with California's marijuana plant. What I mean by legalizing recreational and highly addictive drugs is to put in place the structural means by which these products can be made available to those who wish or need them for medical or addictive reasons. For this to be achieved, we need the expertise of the pharmaceutical industry. The task must be based on the following:

❖ Addictive drugs should be tested for their toxicity.

❖ Determine the "cutting-agent" to dilute drugs.

❖ Allow enough drug purity to get-high--but not overdose.

❖ Sell through pharmacies as are other drugs today.

❖ Make available by doctor's prescription.

❖ Drug addiction must be legally classified as a medical problem and treated as is alcoholism or addiction to pain-killers.

❖ No commercial advertisement should be permitted.

❖ Addictive drugs should be under strict regulations as is the cigarette industry today.

For the coca producers of the Third World:

❖ Better quality of agricultural methods than those used by Colombian coca *campesinos*.

❖ Fair Trade agreements to increase the coca growers income and reduce their perpetual poverty.

❖ Hemp production should be encouraged and used for its diversified products. Hemp pulp can be used for clothing, paper production and for its oil.

The strong arm of economic can have grave effects upon the direct beneficiaries of the war on drugs: the law enforcement drug squads and other agencies, the trial lawyers, the court system's assembly-line trial process, the revolving doors of the federal and state prison system, the street gangs selling drugs in the inner cities, national and international organized crime groups, and terrorist organizations supported by earnings from the drug trade. It would mean the end of the human misery caused by the deaths of many innocent victims of the cartel turf wars. Above all, it would stop criminalizing the already suffering drug addicts and reduce the need for prostitution as a way of supporting a drug habit. This can be accomplished by the present state of deterioration *within* the confines of drug prohibition.

13

IN PLAIN LANGUAGE: DRUG DECRIMINALIZATION

"No drug, not even alcohol causes the fundamental ills of society. If we're looking for the source of our troubles, we shouldn't test people for drugs, we should test them for stupidity, ignorance, greed and love of power."

P.J. O'Rourke

JANUARY 6, 1995
AMERICAN CIVIL LIBERTIES UNION

More and more ordinary people, elected officials, newspaper columnists, economists, doctors, judges and even the Surgeon General of the United States are concluding that the effects of our drug control policy are at least as harmful as the effects of the drugs themselves.

After decades of drug prohibition and intensive drug enforcement efforts to rid the country of illegal drugs, violent traffickers still endanger life in our cities, a steady stream of drug offenders still pours into out jails and prisons, and tons of cocaine, heroin and marijuana still cross our borders unimpeded.

The American Civil Rights Union (ACLU) opposes criminal prohibition of drugs. Not only is drug prohibition a proven failure as a drug control strategy, but it subjects otherwise law-abiding citizens to arrest, prosecution and imprisonment for what they do in private. In trying to enforce the drug laws, the government violates the fundamental rights of privacy and personal autonomy that are guaranteed by our Constitution. The ACLU believes that unless they do harm to others, people should not be punished—even if they do harm to themselves. There are better ways to control drug use, ways that will ultimately lead to a healthier, freer and less crime-ridden society.

CURRENTLY ILLEGAL DRUGS
HAVE NOT ALWAYS BEEN ILLEGAL

During the Civil War, morphine (an opium derivative and cousin of heroin) was found to have pain killing properties and soon became the main ingredient in several patent medicines.

In the late 19th century, marijuana and cocaine were put to various medicinal uses–marijuana to treat migraines, rheumatism and insomnia, and cocaine to treat sinusitis, hay fever and chronic fatigue. All of these drugs were also used recreationally, and cocaine, in particular, was a common ingredient to wines and soda pop–including the popular Coca-Cola.

In 1933, because of concern over widespread organized crime, police corruption and violence, the public demanded repeat of alcohol prohibition and the return of regulatory power to the states. Most states immediately replaced criminal bans with laws regulating the quality, potency and commercial sale of alcohol; as a result, the harms associated with alcohol prohibition disappeared. Meanwhile, federal prohibition of heroin and cocaine remained, and with the passage of the Marijuana Stamp Act in 1937 marijuana was prohibited as well. Federal drug policy has remained strictly prohibitionist to this day.

DECADES OF DRUG PROHIBITION: A HISTORY OF FAILURE

Criminal prohibition, the centerpiece of US drug policy, has failed miserably. Since 1981, tax dollars to the tune of $150 billion have been spent trying to prevent Colombian cocaine, Burmese heroin and Jamaican [and Mexican] marijuana from penetrating our borders. Yet, the evidence is that for every ton seized, hundreds get through. Hundreds of thousands of otherwise law abiding people have been arrested and jailed for drug possession. Between 1968 and 1992, the annual number of drug-related arrests increased from 200,000 to over 1.2 million. One-third of those arrests were for mere possession.

The best evidence of prohibition's failure is the government's current war on drugs. This war, instead of employing a strategy of prevention, research, education and social programs designed to address problems such as permanent poverty, long-term unemployment, and deteriorating living conditions in our inner cities, has employed a strategy of law enforcement. While this military approach continues to devour billions of tax dollars and sends tens of thousands of people to prison, illegal drug trafficking thrives [as does]... unchecked spread of the AIDS virus among drug users, their sexual partners and their offspring.

DRUG PROHIBITION IS A PUBLIC HEALTH MESSAGE

Drug prohibition promises a healthier society by denying people the opportunity to become drug users and possibly, addicts.

No quality control. When drugs are illegal, the government cannot enact standards of quality, purity or potency. Consequently, street drugs are often contaminated or extremely potent, causing disease and sometimes death to these who use them.

Dirty needles. Unspecialized needles are known to transmit HIV among intravenous drug users. Yet drug users share needles because laws prohibiting possession of drug paraphernalia have made needles a scarce commodity....more than 60% of intravenous drug users are HIV positive....the figure is less than 1% in Liverpool, England, where clean needles are easily available.

DRUG PROHIBITION CREATES MORE PROBLEMS THAN IT SOLVES

Drug prohibition has not only failed to curb or reduce the harmful effects of drug use, it has created other serious social problems.

Caught in the crossfire. In the same way that alcohol prohibition fuelled violent gangsterism in the 1920's, today's drug prohibition has spawned a culture of drive-by shootings and other gun-related crimes. And just as most of the 1920's violence was not committed by people who were drunk, most of the drug-related violence is not committed by people who are high on drugs. The killings, then and now, are based on rivalries. A 1989 government study of all 193 "cocaine-related" homicides in New York City found that 87% grew out of rivalries and disagreements related to doing business in an illegal market. In only one case was the perpetrator actually under the influence of cocaine.

A Nation of Jailers. The "lock'em up" mentality of the war on drugs has burdened our criminal justice system to the breaking point. Today, drug-law enforcement consumes more than half of all police resources nationwide, resources that could be better spent fighting violent crimes like rape, assaults and robbery…Non-violent drug offenders make up 58% of the federal prison population, a population that is extremely costly to maintain.

PROHIBITION IS A DESTRUCTIVE FORCE IN THE INNER-CITY COMMUNITIES

Inner city communities suffer the most from both the problems of drug abuse and the consequences of drug prohibition.

Although the rates of drug use among white and non-white [persons] are similar, African Americans and other racial minorities are arrested and imprisoned at higher rates. For example, according to government estimates only 12% of drug users are black, but nearly 40% of those arrested for drug offences are black. Nationwide, one-quarter of young African American men are under some form of criminal justice supervision, mostly for drug offences. This phenomenon has had a devastating social impact in minority communities....

Finally, turf battles among competing drug enterprises, as well as police responses to those conflicts, occur disproportionately in poor communities, making our inner-cities war zones and their residents the war's primary casualties.

DRUGS ARE HERE TO STAY - LET'S REDUCE THEIR HARM

The universality of drug use throughout human history has led some experts to conclude that the desire to alter consciousness, for whatever reasons, is a basic human drive. People in almost all cultures, in every era, have used psychoactive drugs. Native South Americans use peyote and tobacco in their religious ceremonies the way Europeans use wine. Alcohol is the drug of choice in Europe, the U.S. and Canada, while many Muslim countries tolerate the use of opium and marijuana.

A "drug free America" is not a realist goal, and by criminally banning psychoactive drugs the government has ceded all control of potentially dangerous substances to criminals. Instead of trying to stamp out all drug use, our government should focus on reducing drug abuse and prohibition-generated crime. This requires a fundamental change in public policy: repeal of criminal prohibition and the creation of a reasonable regulatory system.

ENDING PROHIBITION WOULD NOT NECESSARILY INCREASE DRUG ABUSE

While it is impossible to predict exactly how drug use patterns would change under a system of regulated manufacture and distribution, the iron rules of prohibition are that 1) illegal markets are controlled by producers, not consumers and 2) prohibition fosters the sale and consumption of more potent and dangerous forms of drugs....

Another factor to consider is the lure of forbidden fruit. For young people, who are often attracted to taboos, legal drugs might be less tempting than they are now. That has been the experience of The Netherlands. After the Dutch government decriminalized marijuana in 1976, allowing it to be sold and consumed openly in small amounts, usage steadily declined - particularly among teenagers and young adults. Prior to the decriminalization, 10% of Dutch 17 and 18 year olds used marijuana. By 1985, that figure had dropped to 6.5% .

Without prohibition, providing help to drug abusers who want to kick their habits would be easier because the money now being squandered on law enforcement could be used for preventive social programs and treatment.

Ending prohibition is not a panacea. It will not by itself end drug abuse or eliminate violence. Nor will it bring about the social and economic revitalization of our inner cities. However, ending prohibition would bring in a very significant benefit: it would sever the connection between drugs and crime that today blights so many lives and communities. In the long run, ending prohibition could foster the redirection of public resources toward social development, legitimate economic opportunities and effective treatment, thus enhancing the safety, health and well-being of the entire society. **What the Reader Can Do !**

The need has never been greater for freedom-loving people to support the American Civil Liberties Union (ACLU).

By making a donation you can make sure that drug pro-hibition is eliminated. For more information please contact: www.actu.org

TRANSNATIONAL INSTITUTE:
A WORLDWIDE FELLOWSHIP OF SCHOLAR ACTIVISTS
SEPTEMBER 1, 2009

ARGENTINA'S SUPREME COURT "ARRIOLA" RULING
on the Possession of Drugs for Personal Consumption

"On August 25, 2009, Argentina's Supreme Court of Justice of Argentina unanimously declared to be unconstitutional the second paragraph of Article 14 of the country's drug control legislation (Law Number 23,737), which punishes the possession of drugs for personal consumption with prison sentences ranging from one month to two years (although education or treatment measures can be substitute penalties). According to the Court, the unconstitutionality of the article is applicable to cases of drug possession for personal consumption that does not affect others.

Argentina's Supreme Court jurisprudence on this issue has oscillated over time. The 1978 "Colavini" ruling, during the country's last military dictatorship, considered criminalities for drug possession for personal consumption to be constitutional. In 1986,...the Court's "Baztemica" ruling reversed "Colavini", declaring criminal penalties for such acts to be unconstitutional. In 1990, the Court's "Moltavlo" ruling overturned "Baztemica" returning to the "Colavini" rationale. The Court's new ruling, known as "Amiola", represents a return to the "Baztemica" framework, although with some limits.

The Court noted! "the second paragraph of article 14 of Law Number 23,737 should be invalidated, since it violates Article 19 of the National Constitution, in the sense that it invades the sphere of personal liberty, which is excluded from the authority of state organs. For that reason, the unconstitutionality of the legal deposition is declared, for it incriminates the possession of drugs for personal use under circumstances that do not bring any concrete danger of harm to the rights and welfare of others." (Supreme Court Judge Elena Highton de Nolasco).

The ruling resolved the case of five people who were apprehended leaving a house that was under investigation for drug sales. They were arrested by police officers just a few meters away from the house, and each one of them was found to be in possession of small quantities of marijuana (more or less three cigarettes each).

The ruling's principal argument is that the law penalizing the possession of drugs for personal consumption, to the extent that it invades the private sphere of individuals, affects the right to privacy, which is protected by constitutional norms (not only article 19 of the Argentine National Constitution but also international human rights instruments incorporated after the 1994 constitutional reform). In this regard, the Court noted that: "drug possession for personal consumption in itself does not provide any reason to affirm that the accused have carried out anything more than a private act or that they have offended public morals or the rights of others".

(Supreme Court Judge Carmen Argibay).

On this point, the judges understood that the right to privacy must take precedence, but they established a limit regarding the constitutional protection when this conduct affects third parties. This leaves a gray area regarding some cases of possession for general consumption, like those in a public are but without anyone close by. In addition to the main argument, the various judges, most of whom wrote their own opinion in the ruling, included other lines of argument.

Supreme Court Judge Carlos Fayt noted: the failure of criminal persecution of drug users as a way to fight drug trafficking. He noted: "Today, the approach of criminalizing drug use is revealing itself to be both ineffective and inhumane" Developing the idea further, he noted, "how clearly ineffective the current strategy, especially the idea that criminal persecution for drug possession for personal consumption would successfully combat drug trafficking." He added, "the old conception that all criminal legislation must be directed inevitably against both the trafficker and the consumer has been proven outdated".

Supreme Court Judge Zaffarini noted: "The criminal sanctioning of drug users...has become an obstacle for the recovery of those few who are drug dependent, since it only serves to stigmatize them and reinforce their identification with drug use, clearly undermining progress in any type of detoxification therapy and change of conduct that seeks precisely to build self-esteem on the base of values other than drug use."

Supreme Court Judge Ricardo Lorenzetti Highton de Nolasco and Fayt underscored that the United Nations drug control conventions do not obligate the Argentine State to penalize drug possession for personal consumption. Judge Lorenzetti pointed out that "none of the conventions subscribed to by the Argentine State in relation to this issue... compel the State to criminalize drug possession for personal use. Rather, it indicates that this issue remains 'subject to the constitutional principle and fundamental concepts...and so the Conventions' regulations easily prove their respect for Article 19 of the Argentine Constitution."

Judges Lorenzetti and Fayt also noted the regional trend to retract the use of criminal law in relation to drug users, with Judge Lorenzetti citing the examples of Brazil, Peru, Chile, and Uruguay.

Referring to drug use, Judge Fayt indicated: "It is clear that defitinitive answer for these questions cannot be found in the framework of criminal law without jeopardising possible solution in other areas. Criminalizing an individual [for drug use] is undeniably inhumane, subjecting the person to a criminal process that will stigmatize him for the rest of his life and subject him, in some cases, to prison time."....

Finally, the Court, going beyond the resolution of the particular case, urged: "All instances of government to ensure a State policy against illicit drug trafficking and to adopt preventative health measures - including information and education to dissuade people from drug use - geared primarily at vulnerable groups, especially minors, in order to adequately comply with the international human rights treaties to which our country subscribes."

The Transnational Institute goes on to say: *"We applauded this attempt of the Supreme Court Judges to distance the criminal law from drug users. However, we believe that attention will have to be paid to how judges in the lower courts apply these criteria, as the limits of the term "effect others" could still be used to incriminate drug users, especially by the police and by some judges reluctant to permit any change of the criminal law. In this sense, we hope that future legislative reforms provide more precision on this matter, given that we have always believed that drug use is a social and health phenomenon and that alternative answers and solutions should be employed, rather than the penal response which, as the Court has said, is "ineffective and inhumane."*

Argentine National Constitution, Article 19:

"Private actions that offend in no way order and public morals, or damage a third party, are exclusively to God, and are exempt from the authority of judges. No inhabitant of the Nation will be obliged to do that which the law does not order, nor be deprived of that which it does not prohibit. "

LAW ENFORCEMENT AGAINST PROHIBITION
PRESS RELEASE : JANUARY 13, 2009

"SEATLE, WA - A Mountlake Terrace police sergeant who was fired after publicly criticizing the war on drugs has reached an $812,000 settlement in a lawsuit he filed against the city and police department, among others. Under the settlement, Sergeant Jonathan Wender has been reinstated on the force and is eligible to receive back pay and full retirement benefits.

"In an open society, people on the front lines of the criminal justice system, have an ethical duty to speak out on controversial social and legal issues that effect the public we serve," said Sgt. Wender, a member of Law Enforcement Against Prohibition (LEAP), a 10,000-strong organization representing police, prosecutors, judges and others who fought on the front lines of the war on drugs and who now want to legitimize and regulate drugs. "The public has a fundamental right to know which laws and policies are effective, and which ones aren't; and they should expect that their police officers

will speak the truth even when it isn't popular or comfortable to do so. I hope that the outcome of this case will help reassure police and other officials that they can speak freely on controversial topics such as the urgent need to seek better ways to deal with the crisis of drugs that plague American society."

"Jonathan Wender's victory is ours as well. As was his fight," said Norm Stamper, the retired Seattle police chief and LEAP member. "Because of this fine man's courage and perseverance, and his willingness to tell the truth about the drug war, we all moved closer to putting an end to that war. I believe police officers across the country will be moved by Jonathan's example, and will raise their voices in support of LEAP's goal of ending drug prohibition."

Show your support for LEAP www.leap.cc

HARM REDUCTION STEPS: VANCOUVER'S INSITE PROGRAM

In 2003, the first legal safe-injection room opened in Vancouver, Canada, where an estimated 700 users a day are provided with clean needles, and are self-administer narcotics under the supervision of nurses. An estimated 15-18 million North Americans are currently using prohibited drugs, using unhygienic paraphernalia, and putting themselves at risk for side effects ranging from HIV and Hepatitis C to cardiac arrest. The most popular of the prohibited hard drugs are cocaine, ecstasy, heroin, LSD, methamphetamine and PCP.

This is a government approved safe injection facility conveniently located in Vancouver's Lower East Side area. The notorious intravenous hard drug problem in this area is readily apparent. Most of the 4,700 injection drug users are located in this Skid Row area, and there are attempts to persuade them all to use the safe-injection rooms. According to the *National Review of Medicine* (June 2004), "We estimate that over 90% have hepatitis C and over one third have HIV." The establishing of a safe injection site is an initial stage in a move away from the old school manner of dealing with drug abuse. The facility is a co-ordinated effort of the City of Vancouver, the police and Vancouver's Coastal Health Authority for Addiction Medicine.

Aside from providing a safe site for drug injection, the facility's nurses may prevent an overdose caused by the lack of quality control in the drugs themselves. During the five years prior to 2003, there were 524 fatal overdoses reported among the 4,700 drug addicts. From 2003 to 2009, nearly two million injection needles were used once and then discarded. Drug users no longer share needles and thus are reducing the threat of contamination. The underlying philosophy is the prevention and spread of HIV and Hepatitis C by providing a sterilized environment for drug users. Users are given a disposable kit with sterilized needles, cookers, tourniquets and filtered water. After injecting, they retreat into a temperature controlled post-injection room before returning to their normal daily lives. In addition, drug users who want to enter a drug rehabilitation program, have on-site access to an addiction counsellor who can process an individual's request for treatment. This is a far better option than back-alley injection and sharing used needles, constant police harassment, robberies and death by overdose. I have witnessed and stepped over discarded needles behind garbage damps, back alleys and hidden doorways, where the next drug user could pick up and re-use contaminated paraphernalia.

Of course, there are those who fear change in the *status quo* in dealing with the social and medical problem of drug use. They are more comfortable with applying a militarized or criminalized approach. In hindsight, the police have reported that this rational control of drug use has significantly reduced the drug-related public nuisance. But let's be clear – shooting galleries are not a drug solution. It is simply a harm reduction of the non-medical use of drugs. It is a stepping-stone to the possibility of educating and helping people to get off drugs. It is beneficial for users and the community, for each prevention of HIV alone saves the community 150 to 220 thousand dollars per year. In short, hard drug users can now get their doses on prescription.

LATIN AMERICA ENACTS DRUG DECRINALIZATION

Many countries in the region, including Mexico, have implemented the decriminalization of small amounts of drugs for personal use. This is also a political objection to the US zero-tolerance stand on possession of all drugs. This is a reversal of a long standing policy by Latin America governments who have implemented US policies in exchange for foreign aid. Now, it appears that many Latin American politicians have begun to repudiate the merits of prohibition, and they are decriminalizing illicit drugs for personal use. To be sure, there are many who still forbid the legalized production, distribution and rational marketing of illicit drugs.

In *Argentina*, a ruling involving marijuana possession cleared the way for the central government to draft a new law decriminalising all drug possession. Currently, possession of small amounts carries no jail time or fines; the user must undergo supervised rehabilitation.

Bolivia has been accused by the US Drug Administration of not fully co-operating with US-mandated eradication of coca production which may rob peasants of their livelihood.

In *Brazil*, the minister of justice and the environmental minister have spoken often and openly against drug prohibition. The minister of justice, Carlos Minc, is expected to fully de-criminalize drugs for personal use. Most often, prison sentences have been replaced by rehabilitation efforts.

Since 1994, *Columbia* has maintained that it is unconstitutional to incarcerate persons who possess small amounts of drugs intended for personal use. It should be noted that such decriminalization is not simply a politician's convenient decision. Rather, it is a legal decision with a national constitutional amendment.

In 2008 *Ecuador* adopted a constitutional referendum to reform drug laws to state that drug possession for personal use should not be penalized. This law goes even further to include reduced sentences for small-scale traffickers, known as mules. Ecuador has also decided to close down the Manta airbase to US operations after more than a decade of use on anti-narcotics operations in the country.

Mexico has decriminalized the amounts of various drugs as follows:

Opium	2 grams	Cocaine	1/2 gram
Heroin	1/10 gram	Marijuana	5 grams
LSD	150 micrograms	Ecstasy	1/5 gram
Methamphetamine	1/5 gram		

It is a recognition that intensifying a military or police war on drugs strategy has proven to be a failure. Since December 2006, more than 15,000 persons have been killed in the prohibition-related violence unleashed by the police, military and the organized drug cartels. However, there is a vast group of persons who still make a living off the small-time trafficking of drugs; however, imprisoning them will not diminish the supply of drugs at the street level. Police corruption is associated with street level junkies, where the cops are control the trafficking of drugs. Something has to be done to give the drug users a break from the corrupt cops.

Paraguay has passed a law legally exempting incarceration for persons caught with 2 grams or less of cocaine or heroin and 10 grams or less of marijuana for personal use.

In *Peru*, possession of small amounts of drug is legal; judges decide what constitutes personal or for sale.

For decades, *Uruguay*, has left criminal sentencing to the judges to determine whether the intention of drug possession is personal use–which is legal–or for sale, which is not.

Venezuela does not appear to co-operate fully with the US escalation of the war on drugs.

The decriminalization of drug possession has gone into effect for over 160 million Latin Americans. What is impressive is that decriminalisation has gone through each country's legislative process and each country's laws criminalizing drug possession has been declared unconstitutional. This is a dramatic shift in drug policy. It permits a distinction between users and organized drug traffickers. It also allows national authorities to focus their efforts on reducing the terrible human misery caused by the drug cartels and the violence associated with the illicit trafficking of drugs. Warehousing small time dope peddlers and users in jails has proven futile. This is very, very significant, for treating drug use and addiction as a public health - not a law enforcement iissue.

EUROPE'S LENIENT LANDS

In Europe, the authorities face the difficulty of enforcement, overloaded courts and overcrowded prisons. The tough laws recommended for drug possession are seldom handed out. Statistics for 2008 show the degree of conviction and sentences for drug possession for personal use:

	Prison	Suspended Sentence	Fines	Community Work	* Other
Austria	5%	75%	5%	0%	15%
France	12%	15%	50%	3%	20%
Germany	8%	15%	75%	0%	2%
Latvia	5%	5%	80%	2%	8%
Poland	5%	45%	35%	13%	2%
Portugal	0%	15%	2%	83%	0%
Slovakia	5%	15%	5%	0%	75%
Croatia	5%	45%	28%	0%	22%
Denmark	5%	2%	90%	0%	3%
Czech Rep.	2%	50%	30%	3%	15%
Britain, Wales	1%	82%	5%	12%	0%
Netherlands	20%	10%	30%	25%	15%

Source: EMCDDA * Warning, treatment orders, prosecutions

As the reader can see, many European countries still impose prison terms as an option for convicted drug users. In reality, however, only a small number end up in jail, according to the above statistics. Right-wing politicians propose longer sentences for serial drug offenders and suspected dealers than the average time of three months.

Here, we must point out that decriminalizing personal possession, though helpful in relieving further human misery, will not do much to tackle the organized crime gangs of South America, the Middle East and Europe. The rational approach is to legalize the supply of drugs, rather than just going easy on drug users.

INDEX

"I'm in favour of legalizing drugs. According to my value system, if people want to kill themselves, they have every right to do so. Most of the harm that comes from drugs is because they are illegal."

Milton Friedman

Abimael Guzman– 3, 140

Addiction– 36-37, 117, 119, 124
Alcoholism– 21, 37, 48, 52
Alcohol prohibition– 2, 8, 12, 26, 58, 61, 78, 120
American Civil Liberties– 216
American Civil War– 54
Argentine Supreme Court– 228
Argentine National Constitution– 122

Blanket Prohibition– 5, 12, 14, 59
Blue Laws– 67
Bolivia– 2, 68, 99, 109, 111, 136, 143, 146, 179
Bootlegging– 55

Canada– 67-68, 114, 120, 148, 166, 179
Campesinos– 24, 138, 176
Cannabis– 9, 29-30, 33, 39, 92, 119, 201
Chile– 82, 108, 110, 111
Coca Cola– 26, 89, 186
Coca leaves– 25, 69, 186
Coca tea– 25, 99
Coca wine– 26, 86, 183
Cocaine– 59, 62, 86, 119
Coffee prohibition– 15-16
Cigarettes– 17, 21
Contraband– 59, 196, 209,

De-cocainized products– 28, 90, 179, 189
Drug Enforcement Agency (DEA)– 1, 126, 145
Drug decriminalization– 40, 82, 201, 108
Drug prohibition– 8, 10, 39, 67, 82, 117, 168

Economics Against Drug Trafficking– 193
Ecuador– 139, 140-141, 143, 172, 203, 229
Energy drinks – see de-cocainized products
Eradication– 142-143, 172

FARC (Colombian Revolutionary Armed Forces)– 143, 190
Fair Trade of Coca Products– 177
Evo Morales– 149, 187

HIV– 120, 148, 171, 218, 227
Habits– 198-199, 213
Harrison Narcotics Act– 57, 59, 67, 155
Harm Reduction Steps– 116, 122, 125, 127, 148, 227
Hashish– 10, 30-31, 97
Hemp– 9, 29
Heroin– 33, 62, 73, 86, 119, 122

Inner-City Communities– 81, 116, 126, 165, 171, 206, 213, 219
InSite Program– see Harm Reduction Steps
Jungle– 112, 137, 140

KKK– 93
Kola Nut– 26, 184-185

Opium– 21, 33, 59, 86

Latin America– 1, 46, 136, 149, 228
Law Enforcement Against Drug Prohibition– 82, 125, 226

Marianni wine– see coca wine
Mate de Coca– see Coca leaves products
Mercenaries– 145, 149, 172, 174
Mexico– 15, 145-146, 172-173, 228
Morphine– 21, 33, 62, 73

Natural stimulants– 8, 24, 29, 33

Paraguay– 229
Pasta de Coca– 70, 139, 176, 203
Peru– 5, 68, 77, 79, 102, 108, 11, 140, 179

Propaganda– 48, 52, 86, 95, 163, 179

Shining Path (Sendero Luminoso)– 3, 108, 111, 145, 174, 203
Smuggling– 17
Spirits– 24

Taboos– 66-67, 150, 195
Teenagers– 38, 202
Temperance Societies– 13, 17, 48, 53, 67, 154
Tobacco prohibition– 15, 17
Transnational Institute– 229
Tupac Amaru (MRTA)– 108, 145

Volstead Act– 15, 56, 153

War on Drugs– 105, 111, 122-123, 125, 130, 134,145, 154,198
Whiskey– 18, 79
Wine– 8, 33